MIWON KWON

ONE PLACE AFTER ANOTHER

SITE-SPECIFIC ART AND LOCATIONAL IDENTITY

THE MIT PRESS • CAMBRIDGE, MASSACHUSETTS • LONDON, ENGLAND

First MIT Press paperback edition, 2004

This book was set in Monotype Grotesque and Rockwell by Graphic Composition, Inc., and was printed and bound in the United States of America.

Library of Congress Cataloging-in-Publication Data

Kwon, Miwon.
One place after another : site-specific art and locational identity / Miwon Kwon.
p. cm.
Includes bibliographical references and index.
ISBN 978-0-262-11265-9 (hc. : alk. paper), 978-0-262-61202-9 (pb)
1. Site-specific art. 2. Art, Modern—20th century. I. Title.

N6490 .K93 2002
709'.04'07—dc21 2001044753

10 9 8 7

For Umma and Appa

CONTENTS

ACKNOWLEDGMENTS

The first incarnation of this book, in the form of a doctoral thesis, was completed in 1998 at the School of Architecture at Princeton University under the guidance of Rosalyn Deutsche, Hal Foster, and Mark Wigley. I am grateful for their encouragement, critical commentaries, and practical wisdom, which set me in the right direction and pushed me forward. Many people during that time and since then gave me opportunities to develop different aspects of the project as papers or lectures. My thanks to Julie Ault, Ron Clark, Sylvie Fortin, Christian Höller, Janet Kaplan, Richard Meyer, Ellen McMahon, Christian Philipp Müller, Andrew Perchuk, Mathias Poledna, Georg Schöllhammer, Do-Ho Suh, Sergio Vega, and especially the editors of *October* for their timely invitations and keen critical responses.

I am also grateful to many artists, curators, critics, arts administrators, colleagues, and friends who shared their insights and experiences or otherwise encouraged me during the period of the book's preparation. Among them, I am especially indebted to David Deitcher, Mark Dion, Karen Dunbar, Russell Ferguson, Joyce Fernandes, Andrea Fraser, Renée Green, Chris Hoover, Mary Jane Jacob, Silvia Kolbowski, Janet Kraynak, Simon Leung, Roy Levin and the faculty, staff, and students of the MFA Program in Visual Art at Vermont College, Mark Linder, James Marcovitz, Iñigo Manglano-Ovalle, Michael Minelli, Karen Paluzzi-Steele, Diane Shamash, Margaret Sundell, Frazer Ward, Connie Wolf, and Lydia Yee.

The final revision of the book was completed at UCLA, where I am fortunate to be surrounded by the most congenial and supportive faculty and staff. I would like to thank in particular Anthony Vidler and Cécile Whiting in the Department of Art History and Mary Kelly and Juli Carson at the School of Art for their nurturing influence. I also extend special thanks to my students at UCLA for their patient and enthusiastic participation in the seminars that helped to reshape this project. Among them, Katie Mondloch and Doris Chon have been diligent research assistants.

The College Art Association supported the early phase of research and writing with its Professional Development Fellowship for Art Historians, and a Faculty Career Development Grant from UCLA allowed me to devote myself fully to the project in its last months. I thank both institutions for their support.

Along with these thanks, I want to register my sense of loss in the premature deaths of Alice Yang, Ernest Pascucci, Jochen Klein, Joe Wood, and Pat Hearn. Although they were not close friends, or curiously because so, their work provided a broad sense of orientation for mine—a fact recognized regrettably in their passing. The future that I can imagine for my generation in various cultural fields is diminished because of their absence.

Special acknowledgment is due two exceptional people in my life: Helen Molesworth for her inestimable friendship, and Doug Ashford, my most intimate interlocutor, for his intellectual challenges as well as his extraordinary capacity for laughter.

Finally, I am grateful to my family. In immeasurable ways, Sowon Kwon and Andre Tchelistcheff have sustained me with spirited support throughout the duration of this study. Their son Sune gave me moments of inexplicable joy when I needed it most. And Seong Kwon remains an inspiration, helping me to keep all things in proper perspective. I would like to dedicate this book to my mother and father. As they have grown accustomed to counseling, worrying about, and cheering for their children from so far away over so many years, I have reciprocally tried to learn to endure geographical distance and physical separation as surmountable obstacles to intimacy. Even during the most intense periods of self-doubt, I felt the grounding power of their good will and love.

ONE PLACE AFTER ANOTHER

INTRODUCTION

Site-determined, site-oriented, site-referenced, site-conscious, site-responsive, site-related. These are some new terms that have emerged in recent years among many artists and critics to account for the various permutations of site-specific art in the present. On the one hand, this phenomenon indicates a return of sorts: an attempt to rehabilitate the criticality associated with the anti-idealist, anticommercial site-specific practices of the late 1960s and early 1970s, which incorporated the physical conditions of a particular location as integral to the production, presentation, and reception of art. On the other hand, it signals a desire to *distinguish* current practices from those of the past—to mark a difference from artistic precedents of site specificity whose dominant positivist formulations (the most well-known being Richard Serra's) are deemed to have reached a point of aesthetic and political exhaustion.

This concern to reassess the relationship between the art work and its site is largely provoked by the ways in which the term "site-specific" has been uncritically adopted as another genre category by mainstream art institutions and discourses. The term is indeed conspicuous in a diverse range of catalogue essays, press releases, grant applications, magazine reviews, and artist statements today; it is applied rather indiscriminately to art works, museum exhibitions, public art projects, city arts festivals, architectural installations; and it is embraced as an automatic signifier of "criticality" or "progressivity" by artists, architects, dealers, curators, critics, arts administrators, and funding organizations.[1] For those who adhere to cooptation as the most viable explanation of the relationship between advanced art, the culture industry, and the political economy throughout the twentieth century, the unspecific (mis)uses of the term "site-specific" are yet another instance of how vanguardist, socially conscious, and politically committed art practices always become domesticated by their assimilation into the dominant culture. And this argument would insist that if the aesthetic and political efficacy of site-specific art has become insignificant or innocuous in recent years, it is because it has been weakened and redirected by institutional and market forces.

But the current efforts to redefine the art-site relationship are also inspired by a recognition that if site-specific art seems no longer viable—because its critical edges have dulled, its pressures been absorbed—this is partly due to the conceptual limitations of existing models of site specificity itself. In response, many artists, critics, historians, and curators, whose practices are engaged in problematizing received notions of site specificity, have offered alternative formulations, such as context-specific, debate-specific, audience-specific, community-specific, project-based.[2] These terms, which tend to slide into one another at different times, collectively signal an attempt to forge more complex and fluid possibilities for the art-site relationship while simultaneously registering the extent to which the very concept of the site has become destabilized in the past three decades or more.

Yet despite these efforts to rethink site specificity, and despite the rise in interest in the artistic developments of the 1960s and 1970s in general, contemporary art discourse still lacks a substantive account of the historical and theoretical "grounds" of site specificity. Consequently, the framework within which we might discuss the artistic merit and/or political efficacy of the various formulations of site specificity, old and new, remains inconclusive.[3] Most importantly, what remain unrecognized, and thus unanalyzed, are the ways in which the very term "site specificity" has itself become a site of struggle, where competing positions concerning the nature of the site, as well as the "proper" relationship of art and artists to it, are being contested.

This book critically examines site specificity not exclusively as an artistic genre but as a problem-idea,[4] as a peculiar cipher of art and spatial politics. In addition to providing analysis and theorization of the various artistic (re)configurations of site specificity, and reevaluating the rhetoric of aesthetic vanguardism and political progressivism associated with them, the book situates the questions concerning the siting of art as a spatio-political problematic. Which is to say, site specificity is here conceived as what art historian Rosalyn Deutsche has called an "urban-aesthetic" or "spatial-cultural" discourse, which combines "ideas about art, architecture, and urban design, on the one hand, with theories of the city, social space, and public space, on the other."[5] Informed by critical urban theory, post-modernist criticism in art and architecture, and debates concerning identity politics and the public sphere, the book seeks to reframe site specificity as the cultural mediation of broader social, economic, and political processes that organize urban life and urban space.

As a point of departure, the first chapter proposes a genealogy of site specificity since the late 1960s. Emerging out of the lessons of minimalism, site-specific art was initially based in a phenomenological or experiential understanding of the site, defined primarily as an agglomeration of the actual physical attributes of a particular location (the size, scale, texture, and dimension of walls, ceilings, rooms; existing lighting conditions, topographical features, traffic patterns, seasonal characteristics of climate, etc.), with architecture serving as a foil for the art work in many instances. Then, through the materialist investigations of institutional critique, the site was reconfigured as a relay or network of interrelated spaces and economies (studio, gallery, museum, art market, art criticism), which together frame and sustain art's ideological system. Works by artists such as Michael Asher, Daniel Buren, Hans Haacke, and Mierle Laderman Ukeles are seen as challenging the hermeticism of this system, complicating the site of art as not only a physical arena but one constituted through social, economic, and political processes.

In more recent site-oriented, project-based art by artists such as Mark Dion, Andrea Fraser, Renée Green, Christian Philipp Müller, and Fred Wilson, among many others, the site of art is again redefined, often extending beyond familiar art contexts to more "public" realms. Dispersed across much broader cultural, social, and discursive fields, and organized intertextually through the nomadic movement of the artist—operating more like an itinerary than a map—the site can now be as various as a billboard, an artistic genre, a disenfranchised community, an institutional framework, a magazine page, a social cause, or a political debate. It can be literal, like a street corner, or virtual, like a theoretical concept. While chapter 1 proposes three paradigms of site specificity—phenomenological or experiential; social/institutional; and discursive—in a somewhat chronological manner, there are no discrete separations or neat periodizing breaks between them. The paradigms are outlined as competing definitions that operate in overlapping ways in past and current site-oriented art.

Chapter 2 examines some key aspects of what the transformation of the site—from a sedentary to a nomadic model—might mean for the art object, artists, and art institutions today. Critical questions concerning the status of originality, authenticity, uniqueness, and authorship, those concepts so central to modernist ideologies of art, which in turn were problematized throughout the 1970s and 1980s, are raised anew in the first section of the chapter. The discussion here takes account of the ways in which the recent trend of reproducing, refabricating, and traveling site-specific art first produced in the late 1960s and early 1970s would seem to betray the earlier premise of site specificity. At the same time, the new conceptual, ethical, and practical problems provoked by this situation force a reorganization of the conventional terms of making, selling, collecting, exhibiting, and distributing site-specific art in both institutional and market contexts. As such, the current mobilization and commodification of site specificity is seen to represent its most salient critical moment even as it enacts a "betrayal" of its earlier aspirations.

The second section of the chapter poses similar questions concerning the status of originality, authenticity, uniqueness, and authorship in relation to the nomadic conditions under which artists pursue new site-oriented practices today. As more artists try to accommodate the increase in demand for singular on-site projects in various cities across the globalized art network (as evidenced, for instance, in the rise in number of city-based biennials and annuals around the world), the definition of site specificity is being reconfigured to imply not the permanence and immobility of a work but its impermanence and transience. The chapter focuses on the impact of this reconfiguration on the role of the artist (now a cultural-artistic service provider rather than a producer of aesthetic objects), the new commodity status of such art "work," and the general shift from the "aesthetics of administration" to the administration of aesthetics in contemporary art. In addition, the chapter reflects on the ways in which such new site-oriented practices accommodate and/or trouble the construction and commodification of urban identities.

Chapter 3 charts the changes in the conceptualization of site specificity within the mainstream public art arena, examining the ways in which an art work's public relevance and its sociopolitical ambitions have been measured in terms of the art-site relationship over the past three decades. The incorporation of site specificity as a programmatic imperative by local, state, and national public art agencies in the mid-1970s encouraged the development of a design team approach in which artists were asked to collaborate with architects in producing or refurbishing public spaces, such as urban plazas, waterfront promenades, neighborhood parks, and office lobbies. The resulting paradigm of art-as-public-spaces, or "place-making," accommodated several ongoing circumstances: the expanded scale of artistic (sculptural) practices of the period, such as those of Scott Burton and Michael Heizer, for instance; the need of public art administrators and city officials to integrate art into the urban environment in a more "accessible" manner; and the accelerated growth of real estate investment and urban redevelopment projects throughout the country. Meant to equalize the creative authority of artists and architects in the design of public spaces, this mode of site specificity presumed the humanizing influence of art over the inhumanity of urban architecture. The ideology of functional utility, foundational to the modernist ethos of architecture and urban design, came to overtake the essentialism of formalist beauty, traditionally associated with art; site-specific public art now needed to be "useful."[6]

Against this backdrop, Richard Serra proposed a countermodel of site specificity with his sculpture *Tilted Arc* (1981–1989). His "medium-differential" approach,[7] in which he uses the language of sculpture to interrogate rather than accommodate the given architecture, disrupted the spatial conditions of the art work's site at Federal Plaza in New York City and challenged the prevailing design-oriented definition of site specificity. The controversy surrounding the removal of *Tilted Arc*—precisely on the point of site specificity's artistic, political, and social validity—is revisited here to establish the terms that become central to public art discourse in subsequent years. John Ahearn's figurative sculptures for a Percent for Art commission in the South Bronx (1991), installed and deinstalled by the artist within one week because of local protest, serves as an important comparative study for the consideration of another alternative model of site specificity. In this case, the site is not simply a geographical location or architectural setting but a network of social relations, a community, and the artist and his sponsors envision the art work as an integral extension of the community rather than an intrusive contribution from elsewhere. The volatile reactions that emerged in response to Ahearn's project, and Ahearn's own response to those reactions, exposed the incommensurate expectations, presumptions, and ideologies at play in much community-based public art today. With the shift from site to community, or the conversion of community into a site, questions concerning the role of the artist, the public function of art, and the definition of community are given new urgency.

Chapter 4 attends more generally to the artistic, architectural, social, and political implications of the shift from site specificity to community specificity in "new genre public art."[8] Claiming a major break from previous approaches to public art, proponents of new genre public art favor temporary rather than permanent projects that engage their audience, particularly groups considered marginalized, as active participants in the conceptualization and production of process-oriented, politically conscious community events or programs. Drawing on a detailed analysis of the highly acclaimed 1993 community-based public art exhibition "Culture in Action" as a case study, this chapter questions the presumptions of aesthetic radicalism, public accessibility, audience empowerment, social relevance, and democracy that support such practice. While many of the goals of new genre public art are salutary, this chapter counters the claims made by many of its advocates that its newness overcomes the contradictions of previous models of site specificity. The chapter unpacks the ways in which new genre public art can exacerbate uneven power relations, remarginalize (even colonize) already disenfranchised groups, depoliticize and remythify the artistic process, and finally further the separation of art and life (despite claims to the contrary).

Tracking the complex exchanges among numerous participants in the planning and presentation of "Culture in Action," the chapter also offers a schematic typology of four "communities" that commonly emerge out of community-based collaborations: community of mythic unity; "sited" communities; temporary invented communities; and ongoing invented communities. Collectively, the categories reveal that despite the effort of many artists, curators, critics, and historians to unify recent trends in public art as a coherent movement, there are numerous inconsistencies and contradictions in the field. For instance, while one community type might require extensive artist and/or institutional involvement, another type remains self-sufficient in overseeing the development of its own project. Further, each category defines a different role for the artist, posing, in turn, alternative renditions of the collaborative relationship. These variations indicate the extent to which the very concept of "community" remains highly ambiguous and problematic in public art today.

This last point is emphasized in the review of the key critiques of community-based art in chapter 5, especially as they pertain to ethical issues of uneven power relations in the triangulated exchange between an artist, a curator-art institution, and a community group. From Hal Foster's critique of its ethnographic working methods, to Grant Kester's claims of its reformist-minded "aesthetic evangelism," to Critical Art Ensemble's complete rejection of it, to Martha Fleming's critique of the critics of community-based art, this chapter reveals the extent to which the identity or definition of a community remains open, like the site, as a scene of political struggle. Relying on the work of feminist social theorist Iris Marion Young on the one hand and French philosopher Jean-Luc Nancy on the other, the chapter argues against the common notion of the community as a coherent and unified social formation—equally valorized by neoconservatives and the liberal left—which often serves exclusionary and authoritarian purposes in the very name of the opposite. Instead, the chapter proposes the idea of community as a necessarily unstable and "inoperative" specter in order to think beyond formulaic prescriptions of community, to open onto an altogether different model of collectivity and belonging. Like the concept of the "public sphere," the community may be seen as a phantom,[9] an elusive discursive formation that, as Nancy puts it, is not a "common being" but a nonessential "being-in-common." Based on this insight, the chapter concludes with a provocation to imagine "collective artistic praxis," as opposed to "community-based art."

In the final chapter, the dissipation of the site in site specificity as described in the previous chapters—the prioritizing of its discursivity, its displacement by the community—is examined in relation to the "dynamics of deterritorialization" as elaborated in architectural and urban spatial discourse. While the accelerated speed, access, and exchange of information, images, commodities, and even bodies is being celebrated in one circle, the concomitant breakdown of traditional temporal-spatial experiences and the accompanying homogenization of places and erasure of cultural differences is being decried in another. The intensifying conditions of spatial indifferentiation and departicularization—that is, the increasing instances of locational *un*specificity—are seen to exacerbate the sense of alienation and fragmentation in contemporary life. Consequently, the nature of the tie between subject/object and location, as well as the interplay between place and space, has received much critical attention in the past two decades' theorization of oppositional cultural practice. For example, Fredric Jameson's "cognitive mapping,"[10] Lucy Lippard's "lure of the local,"[11] Kenneth Frampton's "critical regionalism,"[12] Michel de Certeau's "walking in the city,"[13] and Henri Lefebvre's "production of space,"[14] as ideologically divergent as they may be, are all attempts to theorize the transforming nexus between the subject/object and location.

To this list we should add site specificity as an analogous artistic endeavor. For if the search for place-bound identity in an undifferentiated sea of abstract, homogenized, and fragmented space of late capitalism is one characteristic of the postmodern condition, then the expanded efforts to rethink the specificity of the art-site relationship can be viewed as both a compensatory symptom *and* critical resistance to such conditions. Indeed, the resilience of the concept of site specificity as indicated by its many permutations, with its vague yet persistent maintenance of the idea of singular, unrepeatable instances of site-bound knowledge and experience, manifests this doubleness. Countering both the nostalgic desire for a retrieval of rooted, place-bound identities on the one hand, and the antinostalgic embrace of a nomadic fluidity of subjectivity, identity, and spatiality on the other, this book concludes with a theorization of the "wrong place," a speculative and heuristic concept for imagining a new model of belonging-in-transience. As evidenced throughout the book, this task of imagining altogether new coordinations of art and site is an open-ended predicament. Thus, in its final pages, the book can only conjure the critical capacity of intimacies based on absence, distance, and ruptures of time and space.

Robert Smithson, ***Partially Buried Woodshed***, at Kent State University campus, 1970. (© Estate of Robert Smithson/VAGA, New York; courtesy James Cohan Gallery, New York.)

1

GENEALOGY OF SITE SPECIFICITY

Site specificity used to imply something grounded, bound to the laws of physics. Often playing with gravity, site-specific works used to be obstinate about "presence," even if they were materially ephemeral, and adamant about immobility, even in the face of disappearance or destruction. Whether inside the white cube or out in the Nevada desert, whether architectural or landscape-oriented, site-specific art initially took the site as an actual location, a tangible reality, its identity composed of a unique combination of physical elements: length, depth, height, texture, and shape of walls and rooms; scale and proportion of plazas, buildings, or parks; existing conditions of lighting, ventilation, traffic patterns; distinctive topographical features, and so forth. If modernist sculpture absorbed its pedestal/base to sever its connection to or express its indifference to the site, rendering itself more autonomous and self-referential, thus transportable, placeless, and nomadic, then site-specific works, as they first emerged in the wake of minimalism in the late 1960s and early 1970s, forced a dramatic reversal of this modernist paradigm.[1] Antithetical to the claim, "If you have to change a sculpture for a site there is something wrong with the sculpture,"[2] site-specific art, whether interruptive or assimilative,[3] gave itself up to its environmental context, being formally determined or directed by it.

In turn, the uncontaminated and pure idealist space of dominant modernisms was radically displaced by the materiality of the natural landscape or the impure and ordinary space of the everyday. And the space of art was no longer perceived as a blank slate, a tabula rasa, but a real place. The art object or event in this context was to be singularly and multiply experienced in the here and now through the bodily presence of each viewing subject, in a sensory immediacy of spatial extension and temporal duration (what Michael Fried derisively characterized as theatricality),[4] rather than instantaneously perceived in a visual epiphany by a disembodied eye. Site-specific work in its earliest formation, then, focused on establishing an inextricable, indivisible relationship between the work and its site, and demanded the physical presence of the viewer for the work's completion. The (neo-avant-gardist) aesthetic aspiration to exceed the limitations of traditional media, like painting and sculpture, as well as their institutional setting; the epistemological challenge to relocate meaning from within the art object to the contingencies of its context; the radical restructuring of the subject from an old Cartesian model to a phenomenological one of lived bodily experience; and the self-conscious desire to resist the forces of the capitalist market economy, which circulates art works as transportable and exchangeable commodity goods—all these imperatives came together in art's new attachment to the actuality of the site.

In this frame of mind, Robert Barry declared in a 1969 interview that each of his wire installations was "made to suit the place in which it was installed. They cannot be moved without being destroyed."[5] Similarly, Richard Serra wrote fifteen years later in a letter to the director of the Art-in-Architecture Program of the General Services Administration in Washington, D.C., that his 120-foot, Cor-Ten steel sculpture *Tilted Arc* was "commissioned and designed for one particular site: Federal Plaza. It is a site-specific work and as such not to be relocated. To remove the work is to destroy the work."[6] He further elaborated his position in 1989:

> As I pointed out, *Tilted Arc* was conceived from the start as a site-specific sculpture and was not meant to be "site-adjusted" or . . . "relocated." Site-specific works deal with the environmental components of given places. The scale, size, and location of site-specific works are determined by the topography of the site, whether it be urban or landscape or architectural enclosure. The works become part of the site and restructure both conceptually and perceptually the organization of the site.[7]

Barry and Serra echo one another here. But whereas Barry's comment announces what was in the late 1960s a new radicality in vanguardist sculptural practice, marking an early stage in the aesthetic experiments that were to follow through the

1970s (land/earth art, process art, installation art, conceptual art, performance/body art, and various forms of institutional critique), Serra's statement, spoken twenty years later within the context of public art, is an indignant defense, signaling a crisis point for site specificity—at least for a version that would prioritize the *physical* inseparability between a work and its site of installation.[8]

Informed by the contextual thinking of minimalism, various forms of institutional critique and conceptual art developed a different model of site specificity that implicitly challenged the "innocence" of space and the accompanying presumption of a universal viewing subject (albeit one in possession of a corporeal body) as espoused in the phenomenological model. Artists such as Michael Asher, Marcel Broodthaers, Daniel Buren, Hans Haacke, and Robert Smithson, as well as many women artists including Mierle Laderman Ukeles, have variously conceived the site not only in physical and spatial terms but as a *cultural* framework defined by the institutions of art. If minimalism returned to the viewing subject a physical body, institutional critique insisted on the social matrix of the class, race, gender, and sexuality of the viewing subject.[9] Moreover, while minimalism challenged the idealist hermeticism of the autonomous art object by deflecting its meaning to the space of its presentation, institutional critique further complicated this displacement by highlighting the idealist hermeticism of the space of presentation itself. The modern gallery/museum space, for instance, with its stark white walls, artificial lighting (no windows), controlled climate, and pristine architectonics, was perceived not solely in terms of basic dimensions and proportion but as an institutional disguise, a normative exhibition convention serving an ideological function. The seemingly benign architectural features of a gallery/museum, in other words, were deemed to be coded mechanisms that *actively* disassociate the space of art from the outer world, furthering the institution's idealist imperative of rendering itself and its values "objective," "disinterested," and "true."

As early as 1970 Buren proclaimed, "Whether the place in which the work is shown imprints and marks this work, whatever it may be, or whether the work itself is directly—consciously or not—produced for the Museum, any work presented in that framework, if it does not explicitly examine the influence of the framework upon itself, falls into the illusion of self-sufficiency—or idealism."[10] More than just the museum, the site comes to encompass a relay of several interrelated but different spaces and economies, including the studio, gallery, museum, art criticism, art history, the art market, that together constitute a system of practices that is not separate from but open to social, economic, and political pressures. To be "specific" to such a site, in turn, is to decode and/or recode the institutional conventions so as to expose their hidden operations—to reveal the ways in which institutions mold art's meaning to modulate its cultural and economic value; to undercut the fallacy of art's and its institutions' autonomy by making apparent their relationship to the broader socioeconomic and political processes of the day. Again, in Buren's somewhat militant words from 1970:

> Art, whatever else it may be, is exclusively political. What is called for is the *analysis of formal and cultural limits* (and not one *or* the other) within which art exists and struggles. These limits are many and of different intensities. Although the prevailing ideology and the associated artists try in every way to *camouflage* them, and although it is too early—the conditions are not met—to blow them up, the time has come to *unveil* them.[11]

In nascent forms of institutional critique, in fact, the physical condition of the exhibition space remained the primary point of departure for this unveiling. For example, in works such as Hans Haacke's *Condensation Cube* (1963–1965), Mel Bochner's *Measurement* series (1969), Lawrence Weiner's wall cutouts (1968), and Buren's *Within and Beyond the Frame* (1973), the task of exposing those aspects which the institution would obscure was enacted literally in relation to the architecture of the exhibition space—highlighting the humidity level of a gallery by allowing moisture to "invade" the pristine minimalist art object (a mimetic configuration of the gallery space itself); insisting on the material fact of the gallery walls as "framing" devices by notating the walls' dimensions directly on them; removing portions of a wall to reveal the base reality behind the "neutral" white cube; and ex-

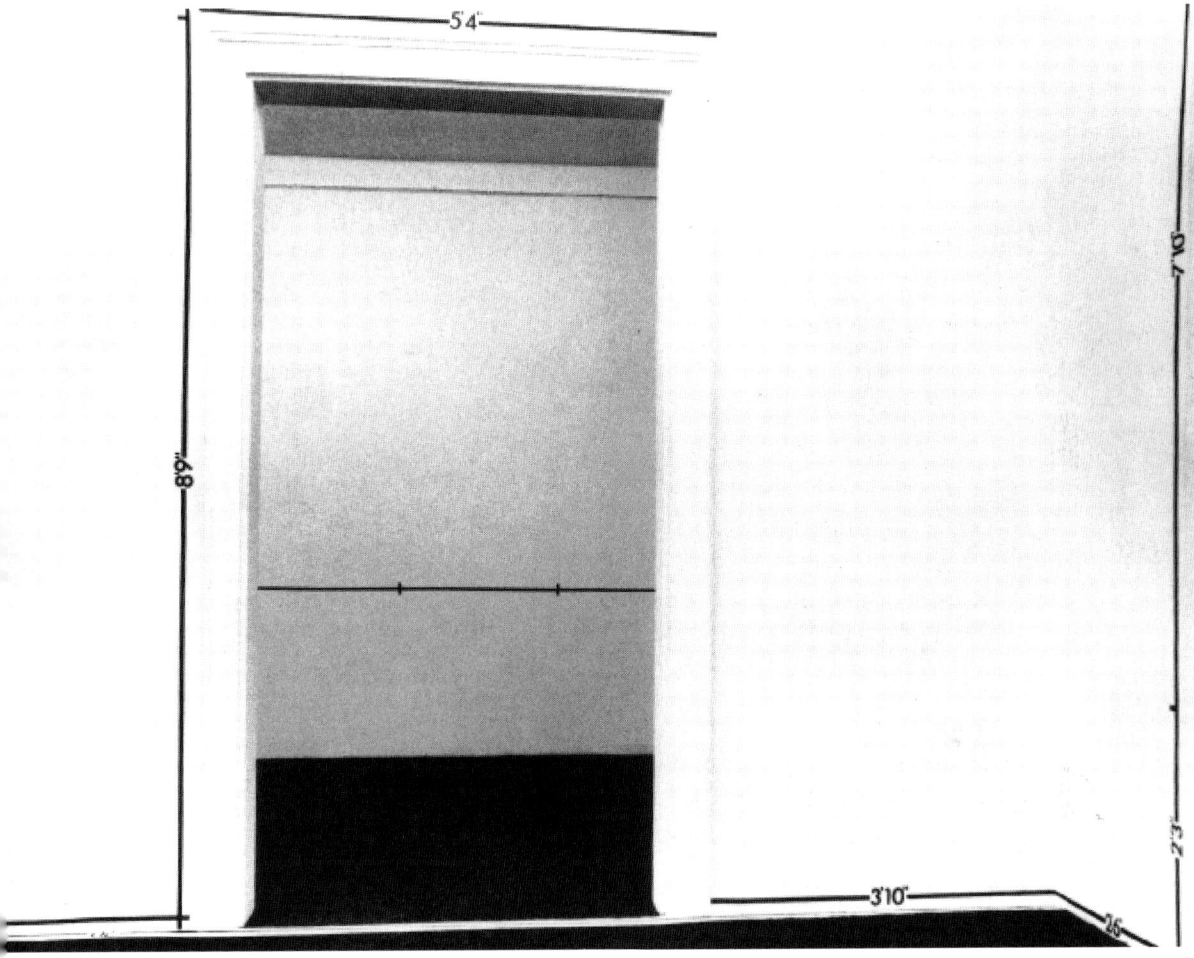

Mel Bochner, ***Measurement: Room***, tape and Letraset on wall, installation at Galerie Heiner Friedrich, Munich, 1969. (Photo by the artist; Collection The Museum of Modern Art, New York.)

Daniel Buren, photo-souvenir: ***Within and Beyond the Frame***, John Weber Gallery, New York, 1973. (© Daniel Buren.)

ceeding the physical boundaries of the gallery by having the art work literally go out the window, ostensibly to "frame" the institutional frame. Attempts such as these to expose the cultural confinement within which artists function—"the apparatus the artist is threaded through"—and the impact of its forces upon the meaning and value of art became, as Smithson had predicted in 1972, "the great issue" for artists in the 1970s.[12] As this investigation extended into the 1980s, it relied less and less on the physical parameters of the gallery/museum or other exhibition venues to articulate its critique.

In the paradigmatic practice of Hans Haacke, for instance, the site shifted

Michael Asher, untitled installation at Claire Copley Gallery, Inc., Los Angeles, 1974. (Photo by Gary Krueger; courtesy the artist.)

from the physical condition of the gallery (as in *Condensation Cube*) to the system of socioeconomic relations within which art and its institutional programming find their possibilities of being. His fact-based exposés through the 1970s, which spotlighted art's inextricable ties to the ideologically suspect if not morally corrupt power elite, recast the site of art as an institutional frame in social, economic, and political terms, and enforced these terms as the very content of the art work.[13] Exemplary of a different approach to the institutional frame are Michael Asher's surgically precise displacement projects, which advanced a concept of site that included historical and conceptual dimensions. In his contribution to the "73rd American Exhibition" at the Art Institute of Chicago in 1979, for instance, Asher revealed the sites of exhibition or display to be culturally specific situations that generate particular expectations and narratives regarding art and art history. Institutional framing of art, in other words, not only distinguishes qualitative value; it also (re)produces specific forms of knowledge that are historically located and culturally determined—not at all universal or timeless standards.[14]

Yet another approach to a critique of the institutional frame is indicated in Mierle Laderman Ukeles's 1973 series of "maintenance art" performances at the Wadsworth Atheneum in Hartford, Connecticut.[15] In two of the performances, Ukeles, literally on her hands and knees, washed the entry plaza and steps of the museum for four hours, then scrubbed the floors inside the exhibition galleries for another four hours. In doing so, she forced the menial domestic tasks usually associated with women—cleaning, washing, dusting, and tidying—to the level of aesthetic contemplation, and revealed the extent to which the museum's pristine self-presentation, its perfectly immaculate white spaces as emblematic of its "neutrality," is structurally dependent on the hidden and devalued labor of daily maintenance and upkeep. By foregrounding this dependence, Ukeles posed the museum as a hierarchical system of labor relations and complicated the social and gendered division between the notions of the public and the private.[16]

In these ways, the site of art begins to diverge from the literal space of art, and the physical condition of a specific location recedes as the primary element in the conception of a site. Whether articulated in political and economic terms, as in

Mierle Laderman Ukeles, ***Hartford Wash: Washing Tracks, Maintenance Outside***, Wadsworth Atheneum, Hartford, 1973. (Photos courtesy Ronald Feldman Fine Arts, New York.)

Mierle Laderman Ukeles, ***Hartford Wash: Washing Tracks, Maintenance Inside***, Wadsworth Atheneum, Hartford, 1973. (Photos courtesy Ronald Feldman Fine Arts, New York.)

Haacke's case, in epistemological terms, as in Asher's displacements, or in systemic terms of uneven (gendered) labor relations, as in Ukeles's performances, it is rather the *techniques* and *effects* of the art institution as they circumscribe and delimit the definition, production, presentation, and dissemination of art that become the sites of critical intervention. Concurrent with this move toward the dematerialization of the site is the simultaneous deaestheticization (that is, withdrawal of visual pleasure) and dematerialization of the art work. Going against the grain of institutional habits and desires, and continuing to resist the commodification of art in/for the marketplace, site-specific art adopts strategies that are either aggressively antivisual—informational, textual, expositional, didactic—or immaterial altogether—gestures, events, or performances bracketed by temporal boundaries. The "work" no longer seeks to be a noun/object but a verb/process, provoking the viewers' *critical* (not just physical) acuity regarding the ideological conditions of their viewing. In this context, the guarantee of a specific relationship between an art work and its site is not based on a physical permanence of that relationship (as demanded by Serra, for example) but rather on the recognition of its unfixed *impermanence,* to be experienced as an unrepeatable and fleeting situation.

But if the critique of the cultural confinement of art (and artists) via its institutions was once the "great issue," a dominant drive of site-oriented practices today is the pursuit of a more intense engagement with the outside world and everyday life—a critique of culture that is inclusive of nonart spaces, nonart institutions, and nonart issues (blurring the division between art and nonart, in fact). Concerned to integrate art more directly into the realm of the social,[17] either in order to redress (in an activist sense) urgent social problems such as the ecological crisis, homelessness, AIDS, homophobia, racism, and sexism, or more generally in order to relativize art as one among many forms of cultural work, current manifestations of site specificity tend to treat aesthetic and art historical concerns as secondary issues. Deeming the focus on the social nature of *art's* production and reception to be too exclusive, even elitist, this expanded engagement with culture favors public sites outside the traditional confines of art both in physical and intellectual terms.[18]

Furthering previous (at times literal) attempts to take art out of the mu-

Group Material, ***DaZiBaos***, poster project at Union Square, New York, 1982. (Photo courtesy the artists.)

seum/gallery space-system (recall Daniel Buren's striped canvases marching out the window, or Robert Smithson's adventures in the wastelands of New Jersey or isolated locales in Utah), contemporary site-oriented works occupy hotels, city streets, housing projects, prisons, schools, hospitals, churches, zoos, supermarkets, and they infiltrate media spaces such as radio, newspapers, television, and the Internet. In addition to this spatial expansion, site-oriented art is also informed by a broader range of disciplines (anthropology, sociology, literary criticism, psychology, natural and cultural histories, architecture and urbanism, computer science, political theory, philosophy) and is more sharply attuned to popular discourses (fashion, music, advertising, film, and television). Beyond these dual expansions of art into culture, which obviously diversify the site, the distinguishing characteristic of today's site-oriented art is the way in which the art work's relationship to the actuality of a location (as site) and the social conditions of the institutional frame (as site) are both subordinate to a *discursively* determined site that is delineated as a field of knowledge, intellectual exchange, or cultural debate. Furthermore, unlike in the previous models, this site is not defined as a *pre*condition. Rather, it is generated by the work (often as "content"), and then verified by its convergence with an existing discursive formation.

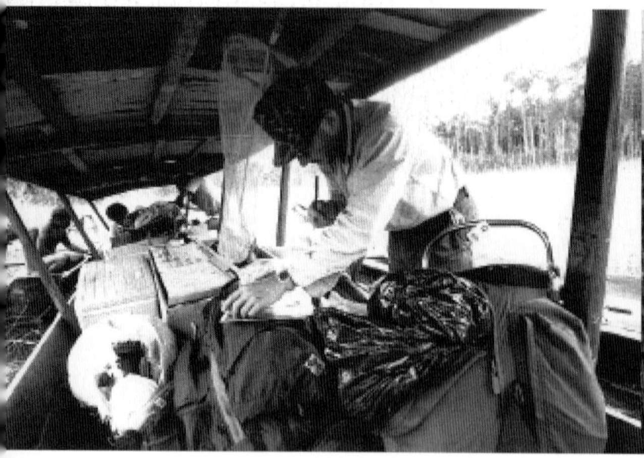

◂ Mark Dion, ***On Tropical Nature***, in the field near the Orinoco River basin, 1991. (Photo by Bob Braine; courtesy American Fine Arts, Co., New York.)

▸ Mark Dion, ***On Tropical Nature***, installation at Sala Mendoza, Caracas, 1991. (Photo by Miwon Kwon.)

Mark Dion, ***New York State Bureau of Tropical Conservation***, with materials from Orinoco River basin reconfigured for installation at American Fine Arts, Co., New York, 1992. (Photo by A. Cumberbirch; courtesy American Fine Arts, Co., New York.)

For example, in Mark Dion's 1991 project *On Tropical Nature,* several different definitions of the site operated concurrently. First, the initial site of Dion's intervention was an uninhabited spot in the rain forest near the base of the Orinoco River outside Caracas, Venezuela, where the artist camped for three weeks collecting specimens of various plants and insects as well as feathers, mushrooms, nests, and stones. These specimens, picked up at the end of each week in crates, were delivered to the second site of the project, Sala Mendoza, one of two hosting art institutions in Caracas. In the gallery space of the Sala, the specimens, which were uncrated and displayed like works of art in themselves, were contextualized within what constituted a third site—the curatorial framework of the thematic group exhibition.[19] The fourth site, however, although the least material, was the site to which Dion intended a lasting relationship. *On Tropical Nature* sought to become a part of the discourse concerning cultural representations of nature and the global environmental crisis.[20]

Sometimes at the cost of a semantic slippage between content and site, other artists who are similarly engaged in site-oriented projects, operating with multiple definitions of the site, in the end find their "locational" anchor in the discursive realm. For instance, while Tom Burr and John Lindell have each produced diverse projects in a variety of media for many different institutions, their consistent engagement with issues concerning the construction and dynamics of (homo)sexuality and desire has established such issues as the "site" of their work. And in many projects by artists such as Lothar Baumgarten, Renée Green, Jimmie Durham, and Fred Wilson, the legacies of colonialism, slavery, racism, and the ethnographic tradition as they impact on identity politics have emerged as an important "site" of artistic investigation. In some instances, artists including Green, Silvia Kolbowski, Group Material, Andrea Fraser, and Christian Philipp Müller have reflected on aspects of site-specific practice itself as a "site," interrogating its currency in relation to aesthetic imperatives, institutional demands, socioeconomic ramifications, or political efficacy.[21] In this way different cultural debates, a theoretical concept, a social issue, a political problem, an institutional framework (not necessarily an art institution), a neighborhood or seasonal event, a historical condition, even particular formations of desire are deemed to function as sites.[22]

This is not to say that the parameters of a particular place or institution no longer matter, because site-oriented art today still cannot be thought or executed without the contingencies of locational and institutional circumstances. But the *primary* site addressed by current manifestations of site specificity is not necessarily bound to, or determined by, these contingencies in the long run. Consequently, although the site of action or intervention (physical) and the site of effects/reception (discursive) are conceived to be continuous, they are nonetheless pulled apart. Whereas, for example, the site of intervention and the site of effect for Serra's *Tilted Arc* were thought of as coincident (Federal Plaza in downtown New York City), Dion's site of intervention (the rain forest in Venezuela or Sala Mendoza) and his projected site of effect (discourse on nature) are distinct. The former clearly serves the latter as material source and inspiration, yet does not sustain an indexical relationship to it.

James Meyer has distinguished this trend in recent site-oriented practice in terms of a "functional site": "[The functional site] is a process, an operation occurring between sites, a mapping of institutional and discursive filiations and the bodies that move between them (the artist's above all). It is an informational site, a locus of overlap of text, photographs and video recordings, physical places and things. . . . It is a temporary thing; a movement; a chain of meanings devoid of a particular focus."[23] Which is to say, the site is now structured (inter)textually rather than spatially, and its model is not a map but an itinerary, a fragmentary sequence of events and actions *through* spaces, that is, a nomadic narrative whose path is articulated by the passage of the artist. Corresponding to the model of movement in electronic spaces of the Internet and cyberspace, which are likewise structured as transitive experiences, one thing after another, and not in synchronic simultaneity,[24] this transformation of the site textualizes spaces and spatializes discourses.

A provisional conclusion might be that in advanced art practices of the past thirty years the operative definition of the site has been transformed from a physical location—grounded, fixed, actual—to a discursive vector—ungrounded, fluid, virtual. Of course, even if a particular formulation of site specificity dominates at one moment and recedes at another, the shifts are not always punctual or definitive. Thus, the three paradigms of site specificity I have schematized here—phenomenological, social/institutional, and discursive—although presented somewhat chronologically, are not stages in a neat linear trajectory of historical development. Rather, they are competing definitions, overlapping with one another and operating simultaneously in various cultural practices today (or even within a single artist's single project). Nonetheless, this move away from a literal interpretation of the site, and the multiple expansions of the site in locational and conceptual terms, seem more accelerated today than in the past. The phenomenon is embraced by many artists, curators, and critics as offering more effective avenues to resist revised institutional and market forces that now commodify "critical" art practices. In addition, current forms of site-oriented art, which readily take up social issues (often inspired by them), and which routinely engage the collaborative participation of audience groups for the conceptualization and production of the work, are seen as a means to strengthen art's capacity to penetrate the sociopolitical organization of contemporary life with greater impact and meaning. In this sense the chance to conceive the site as something more than a place—as repressed ethnic history, a political cause, a disenfranchised social group—is an important conceptual leap in redefining the public role of art and artists.[25]

But the enthusiastic support for these salutary goals needs to be checked by a serious critical examination of the problems and contradictions that attend all forms of site-specific and site-oriented art today, which are visible now as the art work is becoming more and more unhinged from the actuality of the site once again—"unhinged" both in a literal sense of a physical separation of the art work from the location of its initial installation, and in a metaphorical sense as performed in the discursive mobilization of the site in emergent forms of site-oriented art. This unhinging, however, does not indicate a reversion to the modernist autonomy of the siteless, nomadic art object, although such an ideology is still predominant. Rather, the current unhinging of site specificity indicates new pressures upon its practice today—pressures engendered by both aesthetic imperatives and external historical determinants, which are not exactly comparable to those of thirty years ago. For example, what is the status of traditional aesthetic values such as originality, authenticity, and uniqueness in site-specific art, which always begins with the particular, local, unrepeatable preconditions of a site, however it is defined? Is the prevailing relegation of authorship to the conditions of the site, including collaborators and/or reader-viewers, a continuing Barthesian performance of the "death of the author" or a recasting of the centrality of the artist as a "silent" manager/director? Furthermore, what is the commodity status of anticommodities, that is, immaterial, process-oriented, ephemeral, performative events? While site-specific art once defied commodification by insisting on immobility, it now seems to espouse fluid mobility and nomadism for the same purpose. Curiously, however, the nomadic principle also defines capital and power in our times.[26] Is the unhinging of site specificity, then, a form of resistance to the ideological establishment of art, or a capitulation to the logic of capitalist expansion?

Guided by these questions, the next chapter examines two different conditions within which site-specific and site-oriented art have been "circulating" in recent years. First, since the late 1980s, there have been increasing numbers of *traveling* site-specific art works, despite the once-adamant claim that to move the work is to destroy the work. Concurrently, refabrications of site-specific works, particularly from the minimalist and postminimalist eras, are becoming more common in the art world. The increasing trend of relocating or reproducing once unique site-bound works has raised new questions concerning the authenticity and originality of such works as well as their commodity status. Secondly, now that site-specific practices have become familiar (even commonplace) in the mainstream art world, artists are traveling more than ever to fulfill institutional/cultural critique projects in situ. The extent of this mobilization of the *artist* radically redefines the commodity status of the art work, the nature of artistic authorship, and the art-site relationship.

▲ Barry Le Va, ***Continuous and Related Activities: Discontinued by the Act of Dropping*** (1967), felt and glass, installation at Newport Harbor Art Museum, California, 1982. (Photo courtesy Sonnabend Gallery, New York.)

▼ Barry Le Va, ***Continuous and Related Activities: Discontinued by the Act of Dropping*** (1967), felt and glass, reconstructed for the exhibition "The New Sculpture 1965–75: Between Geometry and Gesture" at the Whitney Museum, New York, 1990. (Collection of the Whitney Museum of American Art; Purchase, with funds from the Painting and Sculpture Committee.)

2

UNHINGING OF SITE SPECIFICITY

Mobilization of Site Specificity

The "unhinging" of art works first realized in the 1960s and 1970s is provoked not so much by aesthetic imperatives as by pressures of the museum culture and the art market. Photographic documentation and other materials associated with site-specific art (preliminary sketches and drawings, field notes, instructions on installation procedures, etc.) have long been standard fare in museum exhibitions and a staple of the art market. In the recent past, however, as the cultural and market values of such works from the 1960s and 1970s have risen, many of the early precedents in site-specific art, once deemed difficult to collect and impossible to reproduce, have reappeared in several high-profile exhibitions, such as "L'art conceptuel, une perspective" at the Musée d'art moderne de la ville de Paris (1989) and "The New Sculpture 1965–75: Between Geometry and Gesture" (1990) and "Immaterial Objects" (1991–1992), both at the Whitney Museum.[1]

For exhibitions like these, site-specific works from decades ago are being relocated or refabricated from scratch at or near the location of their re-presentation, either because shipping is too difficult and costly or because the originals are too fragile, in disrepair, or no longer in existence. Depending on the circumstances, some of these refabrications are destroyed after the specific exhibitions for which they are produced; in other instances, the recreations come to coexist with or replace the old, functioning as *new* originals (some even finding homes in permanent collections of museums).[2] With the cooperation of the artist in many cases, art audiences are now being offered the "real" aesthetic experiences of site-specific copies.

The chance to view again such "unrepeatable" works as Richard Serra's *Splash Piece: Casting* (1969–1970), Barry Le Va's *Continuous and Related Activities: Discontinued by the Act of Dropping* (1967), or Alan Saret's *Sulfur Falls* (1968) offers

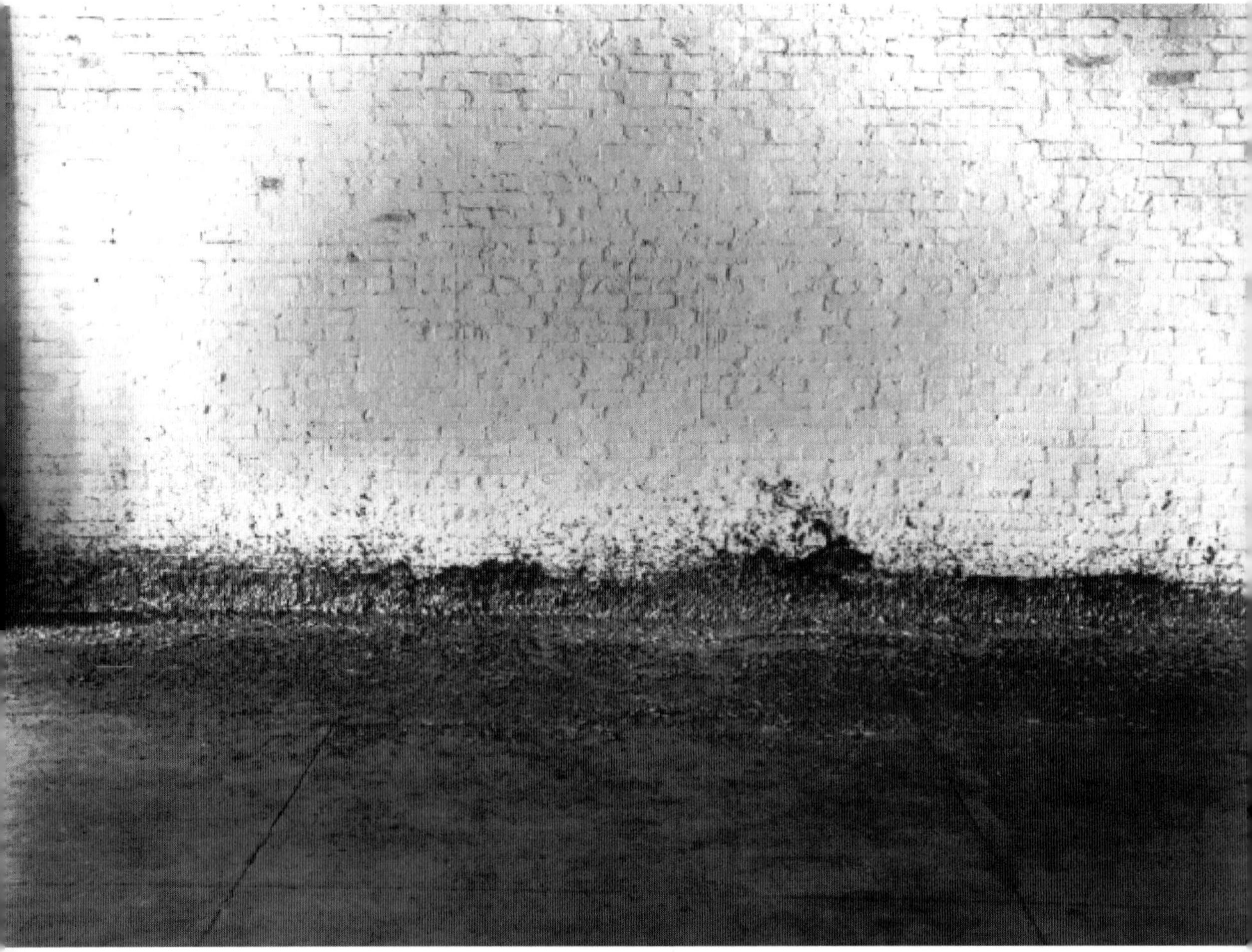

◂ Richard Serra, ***Splashing***, lead, at Castelli Warehouse, New York, 1968. (© Richard Serra/Artists Rights Society (ARS), New York; courtesy Leo Castelli Gallery, New York.)

▸ Richard Serra, ***Splash Piece: Casting*** (1969–1970), lead, at the Whitney Museum of American Art, New York, 1990 (destroyed). (Photo courtesy the artist.)

◂ Richard Serra, ***Splash Piece: Casting*** (1969–1970), lead, at the Museum of Contemporary Art, Los Angeles, 1990 (destroyed). (Photo courtesy the artist.)

▸ Richard Serra, ***Gutter Corner Splash: Night Shift***, installed at the San Francisco Museum of Modern Art, 1995. (Photo by Ivory Serra; The Collection of the San Francisco Museum of Modern Art, Gift of Jasper Johns.)

an opportunity to reconsider their historical significance, especially in relation to the current fascination with the late 1960s and 1970s in art and criticism. But the very process of institutionalization and the attendant commercialization of site-specific art also overturn the principle of place-boundedness through which such works developed their critique of the ahistorical autonomy of the art object. Of course, with much of postminimal, proto-conceptual art work under consideration, there is an ambiguity between ephemerality and site specificity; but both asserted unrepeatability, which is the point I am stressing here.[3] Contrary to the earlier conception of site specificity, the current museological and commercial practices of refabricating (in order to travel) once site-bound works make transferability and mobilization new norms for site specificity. As Susan Hapgood has observed, "the once-popular term 'site-specific,' has come to mean 'movable under the right circumstances,'"[4] shattering the dictum that "to remove the work is to destroy the work."

The consequences of this conversion, effected by object-oriented *de*contextualizations in the guise of historical *re*contextualizations, are a series of normalizing reversals in which the specificity of the site in terms of time and space is rendered irrelevant, making it all the easier for autonomy to be smuggled back into the art work, with the artist allowed to regain his/her authority as the primary source of the work's meaning. The art work is newly objectified (and commodified), and site specificity is redescribed as the personal aesthetic choice of an artist's *stylistic* preference rather than a structural reorganization of aesthetic experience.[5] Thus, a methodological principle of artistic production and dissemination is recaptured as content; active processes are transformed into inert art objects once again. In this way, site-specific art comes to *represent* criticality rather than performing it. The "here and now" of aesthetic experience is isolated as the signified, severed from its signifier.

If this phenomenon represents another instance of domestication of vanguardist works by the dominant culture, it is not solely because of the self-aggrandizing needs of the institution nor the profit-driven nature of the market. Artists, no matter how deeply convinced of their anti-institutional sentiment or how adamant their critique of dominant ideology, are inevitably engaged, self-servingly or with ambivalence, in this process of cultural legitimation. For example, in spring 1990 Carl Andre and Donald Judd both wrote letters of indignation to *Art in America* to publicly disavow authorship of sculptures attributed to them that were included in a 1989 exhibition at the Ace Gallery in Los Angeles.[6] The works in question were recreations: of Andre's 49-foot-long steel sculpture *Fall* from 1968 and of an untitled iron wall piece by Judd of 1970, both from the Panza Collection.[7] Due to the difficulties and high cost of crating and shipping such large-scale works from Italy to California, Panza gave permission to the organizers of the exhibition to refabricate them locally following detailed instructions. As the works had been industrially produced in the first place, the participation of the artists in the refabrication process seemed of little consequence to the director of the Ace Gallery and to Panza. The artists, however, felt otherwise. Not having been consulted on the (re)production and installation of these surrogates, they denounced the refabrications as "a gross falsification" and a "forgery," despite the fact that the sculptures appeared identical to the "originals" in Italy and were reproduced as one-time exhibition copies, not to be sold or exhibited elsewhere.

More than merely a case of ruffled artistic egos, this incident exposes a crisis concerning the status of authorship and authenticity as site-specific art from years ago finds new contexts today. For Andre and Judd, what made the refabricated works illegitimate was not that each was a reproduction of a singular work installed in Varese, Italy, which in principle cannot be reproduced anywhere else anyway, but that the artists themselves did not authorize or oversee the refabrication in California. In other words, the recreations are inauthentic not because of the missing site of their original installation but because of the absence of the artists in the process of their (re)production. By reducing visual variations within the art work to the point of obtuse blankness, and by adopting modes of industrial production, minimal art had voided the traditional standards of aesthetic distinction based on the handiwork of the artist as the signifier of authenticity. However, as the Ace Gallery case amply reveals, despite the withdrawal of such signifiers, authorship and authenticity remain in site-specific art as a function of the artist's "presence" at

Carl Andre, ***Fall*** (1968), installed at the Guggenheim Museum SoHo for the exhibition "Selections from the Guggenheim Museum," 1992. (Photo by David Heald, © The Solomon R. Guggenheim Foundation, New York, Panza Collection.)

the point of (re)production. That is, with the evacuation of "artistic" traces, the artist's *authorship* as producer of objects is reconfigured as his/her *authority to authorize* in the capacity of director or supervisor of (re)production. The guarantee of authenticity is finally the artist's sanction, which may be articulated by his/her actual presence at the moment of production-installation or via a certificate of verification.[8]

While Andre and Judd once problematized authorship through the recruitment of serialized industrial production, only to cry foul years later when their proposition was taken to one of its logical conclusions,[9] artists whose practices are based in modes of "traditional" manual labor have registered a more complex un-

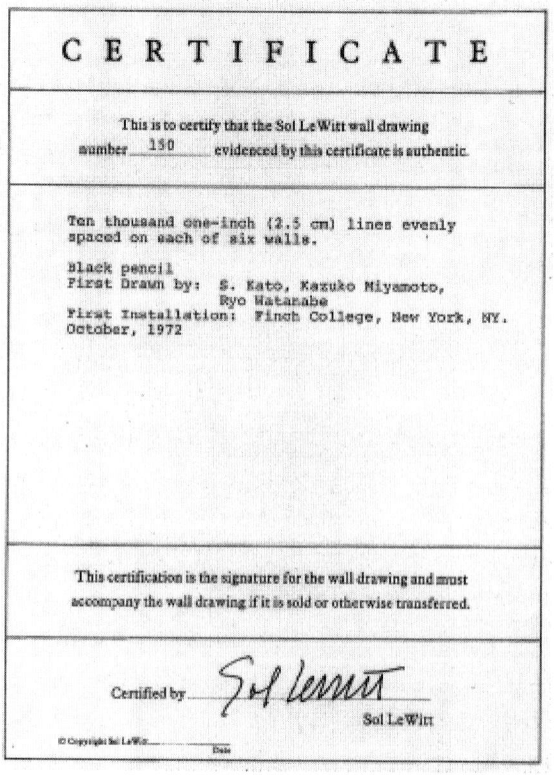

CERTIFICATE

This is to certify that the Sol LeWitt wall drawing
number 150 evidenced by this certificate is authentic.

Ten thousand one-inch (2.5 cm) lines evenly
spaced on each of six walls.

Black pencil
First Drawn by: S. Kato, Kazuko Miyamoto,
Ryo Watanabe
First Installation: Finch College, New York, NY.
October, 1972

This certification is the signature for the wall drawing and must
accompany the wall drawing if it is sold or otherwise transferred.

Certified by Sol LeWitt
Sol LeWitt

© Copyright Sol LeWitt
Date

Sol LeWitt, certificate for ***Wall Drawing no. 150***, October 1972. (Courtesy The Solomon R. Guggenheim Foundation, New York, Panza Collection.)

derstanding of the *politics* of authorship. A case in point: for a 1995 historical survey of feminist art entitled "Division of Labor: 'Women's Work' in Contemporary Art" at the Bronx Museum, Faith Wilding, an original member of the Feminist Art Program at the California Institute of the Arts, was invited to recreate her room-sized site-specific installation *Womb Room (Crocheted Environment)* from the 1972 Womanhouse project in Los Angeles. As the original piece no longer existed, the project presented Wilding with a number of problems, least of which were the long hours and intensive physical labor required to complete the task. To decline the invitation to redo the piece for the sake of preserving the integrity of the original installation would have been an act of self-marginalization, contributing to a self-silencing that would write Wilding and an aspect of feminist art out of the dominant account of art history (again). But on the other hand, to recreate the work as an independent art object for a white cubic space in the Bronx Museum also meant voiding the meaning of the work as it was first established in relation to the site of its original context. Indeed, while the cultural legitimation as represented by the institutional interest in Wilding's work allowed for the (temporary) unearthing of one of the neglected trajectories of feminist art, in the institutional setting of the Bronx Museum and later the Museum of Contemporary Art in Los Angeles, *Womb Room (Crocheted Environment)* became for the most part a beautiful but innocuous work, its primary interest formal, the handicraft nature of the work rendered thematic (feminine labor).[10]

But even if the efficacy of site-specific art from the past seems to weaken when it is re-presented, the procedural complications, ethical dilemmas, and pragmatic headaches that such situations raise for artists, collectors, dealers, and host institutions are still meaningful. They present an unprecedented strain on established patterns of (re)producing, exhibiting, borrowing/lending, purchasing/selling, and commissioning/executing art works in general. At the same time, while some artists regress into the traditional argument of authorial inviolability in order to defend their site-specific practice, others are keen to undo the presumption of criticality associated with such principles as immobility, permanence, and unrepeatability. Rather than resisting mobilization, these artists are attempting to reinvent site specificity as a *nomadic* practice.

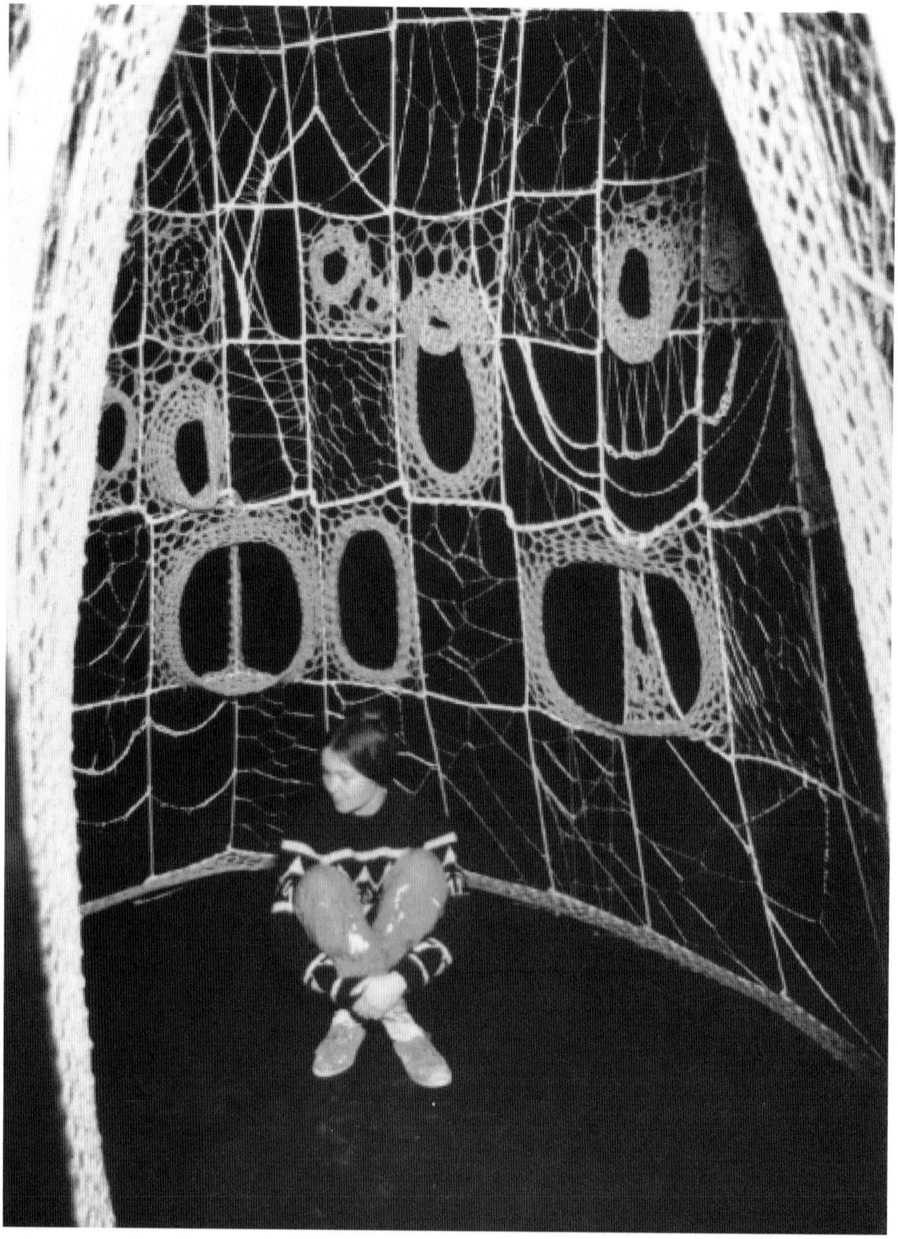

◄ Faith Wilding, ***Womb Room (Crocheted Environment)***, installed at Womanhouse, Los Angeles, 1972. (Photo by Lloyd Hamrol; courtesy the artist.)

► Faith Wilding, ***Womb Room (Crocheted Environment)***, reconstructed for the exhibition "Division of Labor: 'Women's Work' in Contemporary Art" at the Bronx Museum, 1995. (Photo by Becket Logan; courtesy Bronx Museum of Art.)

The increasing institutional interest in current site-oriented practices that mobilize the site as a discursive narrative is demanding an intensive physical mobilization of the artist to create works in various cities throughout the cosmopolitan art world. Typically, an artist (no longer a studio-bound object maker; primarily working now on call) is invited by an art institution to produce a work specifically configured for the framework provided by the institution (in some cases the artist may solicit the institution with a proposal). Subsequently, the artist enters into a contractual agreement with the host institution for the commission. There follow repeated visits to or extended stays at the site; research into the particularities of the institution and/or the city within which it is located (its history, constituency of the [art] audience, the installation space); consideration of the parameters of the exhibition itself (its thematic structure, social relevance, other artists in the show); and many meetings with curators, educators, and administrative support staff, who may all end up "collaborating" with the artist to produce the work. The project will likely be time-consuming and in the end will have engaged the "site" in a multitude of ways, and the documentation of the project will take on another life within the art world's publicity circuit, which will in turn alert another institution to suggest another commission.

Thus, if the artist is successful, he or she travels constantly as a freelancer, often working on more than one site-specific project at a time, globetrotting as a guest, tourist, adventurer, temporary in-house critic, or pseudo-ethnographer[11] to São Paulo, Paris, Munich, London, Chicago, Seoul, New York, Amsterdam, Los Angeles, and so on.[12] Generally, the in situ configuration of a project that emerges out of such a situation is temporary, ostensibly unsuitable for re-presentation anywhere else without altering its meaning, partly because the commission is defined by a unique set of geographical and temporal circumstances and partly because the project is dependent on unpredictable and unprogrammable on-site relations. But such conditions, despite appearances to the contrary, do not circumvent or even complicate the problem of commodification, because there is a strange reversal now by which the artist comes to approximate the "work," instead of the other way around as is commonly assumed (that is, art work as surrogate of the artist). Perhaps because of the absence of the artist from the physical manifestation of the work, the presence of the artist has become an absolute prerequisite for the execution/presentation of site-oriented projects. It is now the *performative* aspect of an artist's characteristic mode of operation (even when working in collaboration) that is repeated and circulated as a new art commodity, with the artist him/herself functioning as the primary vehicle for its verification, repetition, and circulation.[13]

For example, after a yearlong engagement with the Maryland Historical Society, Fred Wilson finalized his site-specific project *Mining the Museum* (1992) as a temporary reorganization of the institution's permanent collection. As a timely convergence of institutional museum critique and multicultural identity politics, *Mining the Museum* drew many new visitors to the Society, and the project received high praise from both the art world and the popular press.[14] Subsequently, Wilson performed a similar archival excavation/intervention at the Seattle Art Museum in 1993, a project also defined by the museum's permanent collection.[15] Although the shift from Baltimore to Seattle, from a historical society to an art museum, introduced new variables and challenges, the Seattle project established a repetitive pattern between the artist and the hosting institution, reflecting what has become a familiar museological practice—the commissioning of artists to rehang permanent collections.[16] The fact that Wilson's project in Seattle fell short of the Baltimore success may be evidence of how ongoing repetition of such commissions can render methodologies of critique rote and generic. They can easily become extensions of the museum's own self-promotional apparatus, while the artist becomes a commodity with a special purchase on "criticality." As Isabelle Graw has noted, "the result can be an absurd situation in which the commissioning institution (the museum or gallery) turns to an artist as a person who has the legitimacy to point out the contradictions and irregularities of which they themselves disapprove." And for artists, "subversion in the service of one's own convictions finds easy transition into subversion for hire; 'criticism turns into spectacle.'"[17]

To say, however, that this changeover represents the commodification of the

Christian Philipp Müller, ***Illegal Border Crossing between Austria and Czechoslovakia***, Austrian contribution to the Venice Biennale, 1993. (Photo courtesy the artist.)

artist is not completely accurate, because it is not the figure of the artist per se, as a personality or a celebrity (à la Warhol), that is produced/consumed in an exchange with the institution. What the current pattern points to, in fact, is the extent to which the very nature of the commodity as a cipher of production and labor relations is no longer bound to the realm of manufacturing (of things) but defined in relation to the service and management industries.[18] The artist as an overspecialized aesthetic object maker has been anachronistic for a long time already. What they *provide* now, rather than *produce,* are aesthetic, often "critical-artistic," services. Andrea Fraser's 1994–1995 project in which she contracted herself out to the EA-Generali Foundation in Vienna (an art association established by companies belonging to the EA-Generali insurance group) as an artist/consultant to provide "interpretive" and "interventionary" services to the foundation, is a uniquely self-conscious playing out of this shift.[19] Through this and prior performance pieces, Fraser highlights the changing conditions of artistic production and reception in terms of both the content and the structure of the project.

Andrea Fraser, ***Museum Highlights: A Gallery Talk***, performance at the Philadelphia Museum of Art, 1989. (Photo by Kelly & Massa; courtesy the artist and American Fine Arts, Co., New York.)

Thus, if Richard Serra could once distill the nature of artistic activities down to their elemental physical actions (to drop, to split, to roll, to fold, to cut, etc.),[20] the situation now demands a different set of verbs: to negotiate, to coordinate, to compromise, to research, to promote, to organize, to interview. This shift was forecast in conceptual art's adoption of what Benjamin Buchloh has described as the "aesthetics of administration."[21] The salient point here is how quickly this aesthetics of administration, developed in the 1960s and 1970s, has converted to the administration of aesthetics in the 1980s and 1990s. Generally speaking, the artist used to be a maker of aesthetic objects; now he/she is a facilitator, educator, coordinator, and bureaucrat. Additionally, as artists have adopted managerial functions of art institutions (curatorial, educational, archival) as an integral part of their creative process, managers of art within art institutions (curators, educators, public program directors), who often take their cues from these artists, now see themselves as authorial figures in their own right.[22]

Concurrent with, or because of, these methodological and procedural changes, there is a reemergence of the centrality of the artist as the progenitor of meaning. This is true even when authorship is deferred to others in collaborations, or when the institutional framework is self-consciously integrated into the work, or when an artist problematizes his/her own authorial role. On the one hand, this "return of the author" results from the thematization of discursive sites, which engenders a misrecognition of them as natural extensions of the artist's identity, and the legitimacy of the work's critique is measured by the proximity of the artist's personal association (converted to expertise) with a particular place, history, discourse, identity, etc. (converted to content). On the other hand, because the signifying chain of site-oriented art is constructed foremost by the movement and decision of the artist,[23] the (critical) elaboration of the project inevitably unfolds around the artist. That is, the intricate orchestration of literal and discursive sites that make up a nomadic narrative *requires* the artist as a narrator-protagonist. In some cases, this renewed focus on the artist in the name of authorial self-reflexivity leads to a hermetic implosion of (auto)biographical and subjective indulgences.

This being so, one of the narrative trajectories of all site-oriented projects is consistently aligned with the artist's prior projects executed in other places, generating what might be called another "site"—the exhibition history of an artist, his/her vitae. The tension between the intensive mobilization of the artist and the recentralization of meaning around him/her is addressed in Renée Green's 1993 *World Tour,* a group reinstallation of four site-specific projects produced in disparate parts of the world over a period of three years.[24] By bringing several distinct projects together, *World Tour* sought to reflect on the problematic conditions of present-day site specificity, such as the ethnographic predicament of artists who are frequently imported by foreign institutions and cities as expert/exotic visitors. *World Tour* also attempted to imagine a productive convergence between specificity and mobility, in which a project created under one set of circumstances might be redeployed in another without losing its impact—or, better, might find new meaning and gain critical sharpness through recontextualizations.[25] But these concerns were not readily available to viewers of *World Tour,* whose interpretive reaction was to see the artist as the primary link between the projects. Indeed, the effort to resituate the individual site-oriented projects as a conceptually coherent ensemble eclipsed the specificity of each and forced a relational dynamic between discrete projects. Consequently, especially for an audience unfamiliar with Green's practice, the overriding narrative of *World Tour* became Green's creative process as an artist in and through the four installations. And in this sense, the project functioned institutionally as a fairly conventional retrospective.

Just as shifts in the structural organization of cultural production alter the form of the art commodity (as service) and the authority of the artist (as primary narrator and protagonist), values like originality, authenticity, and singularity are also reworked in site-oriented art—evacuated from the art work and attributed to the site—reinforcing a general cultural valorization of places as the locus of authentic experience and coherent sense of historical and personal identity.[26] An instructive example of this phenomenon is "Places with a Past," a 1991 site-specific exhibition organized by independent curator Mary Jane Jacob, which took the city of Charleston, South Carolina, as not only its backdrop but "the bridge between the works of art and the audience."[27] In addition to breaking the rules of the art establishment, the exhibition wanted to further a dialogue between art and the socio-historical dimension of the place.[28] According to Jacob, "Charleston proved to be fertile ground" for the investigation of issues concerning "gender, race, cultural identity, considerations of difference . . . subjects much in the vanguard of criticism and art-making. . . . The actuality of the situation, the fabric of the time and place of Charleston, offered an incredibly rich and meaningful context for the making and siting of publicly visible and physically prominent installations that rang true in [the artists'] approach to these ideas."[29]

While site-specific art is still described as refuting originality and authenticity as intrinsic qualities of the art object or the artist, these qualities are readily relocated from the art work to the place of its presentation—only to return to the art work now that it has become integral to the site. Admittedly, according to Jacob, "locations . . . contribute a specific identity to the shows staged by injecting into the experience the uniqueness of the place."[30] Conversely, if the social, historical, and geographical specificity of Charleston offered artists a unique opportunity to create unrepeatable works (and by extension an unrepeatable exhibition), then the programmatic implementations of site-specific art in projects like "Places with a Past" ultimately utilize art to promote Charleston as a unique place. What is prized most of all in site-specific art is still the singularity and authenticity that the presence of the artist seems to guarantee, not only in terms of the presumed unrepeatability of the work but in the way the presence of the artist also endows places with a "unique" distinction.

Certainly, site-specific art can lead to the unearthing of repressed histories, help provide greater visibility to marginalized groups and issues, and initiate the re(dis)covery of "minor" places so far ignored by the dominant culture. But inasmuch as the current socioeconomic order thrives on the (artificial) production and (mass) consumption of difference (for difference sake), the siting of art in "real" places can also be a means to *extract* the social and historical dimensions of these places in order to variously serve the thematic drive of an artist, satisfy institutional demographic profiles, or fulfill the fiscal needs of a city. It is within this framework, in which art serves to generate a sense of authenticity and uniqueness of place for quasi-promotional agendas, that I understand the goals of city-based international art programs like "Sculpture. Projects in Münster 1997." According to its cocurator Klaus Bussmann,

> The fundamental idea behind the exhibitions was to create a dialogue between artists, the town and the public, in other words, to encourage the artists to create projects that dealt with conditions in the town, its architecture, urban planning, its history and the social structure of society in the town. . . . Invitations to artists from all over the world to come to Münster for the sculpture project, to enter into a debate with the town, have established a tradition which will not only be continued in the year 1997 but beyond this will become something specific to Münster: a town not only as an "open-air museum for modern art" but also as a place for a natural confrontation between history and contemporary art. . . . The aim of the exhibition "Sculpture. Projects in Münster" is to make the town of Münster comprehensible as a complex, historically formed structure exactly in those places that make it stand out from other towns and cities.[31]

Significantly, the appropriation of site-specific art for the valorization of urban identities comes at a time of a fundamental cultural shift in which architecture and urban planning, formerly the primary media for expressing a vision of the city, are displaced by other media more intimate with marketing and advertising. In the words of urban theorist Kevin Robins, "As cities have become ever more equivalent and urban identities increasingly 'thin,' . . . it has become necessary to employ advertising and marketing agencies to manufacture such distinctions. It is a question of distinction in a world beyond difference."[32] Site specificity in this context finds new importance because it supplies distinction of place and uniqueness of locational identity, highly seductive qualities in the promotion of towns and cities within the competitive restructuring of the global economic hierarchy. Thus, site specificity remains inexorably tied to a process that renders the particularity and identity of various cities a matter of product differentiation. Indeed, the exhibition catalogue for "Places with a Past" was a "tasteful" tourist promotion, pitching the city of Charleston as a unique, "artistic," and meaningful place (to visit).[33] Under the pretext of their articulation or resuscitation, site-specific art can be mobilized to expedite the erasure of differences via the commodification and serialization of places.

The yoking together of the myth of the artist as a privileged source of originality with the customary belief in places as ready reservoirs of unique identity belies the compensatory nature of such a move. For this collapse of the artist and the site reveals an anxious cultural desire to assuage the sense of loss and vacancy that pervades both sides of this equation. In this sense, Craig Owens was perhaps correct to characterize site specificity as a melancholic discourse and practice,[34] as was Thierry de Duve in claiming that "sculpture in the last 20 years is an attempt to reconstruct the notion of site from the standpoint of having acknowledged its disappearance."[35] Keeping this sense of loss of place or disappearance of the site in mind, we will next turn to the problem of site specificity as it has evolved quite distinctly in the mainstream public art context over the past three decades. We will return to a consideration of site specificity in relation to issues concerning locational identity in the final chapter.

Cover and inside page from the exhibition catalogue ***Places with a Past: Site-Specific Art at Charleston's Spoleto Festival***, 1991.

3

SITINGS OF PUBLIC ART: INTEGRATION VERSUS INTERVENTION

At the juncture of Jerome and Gerard avenues and 169th Street in the South Bronx, across from the 44th Police Precinct building on one side and facing the elevated subway tracks cutting through the sky on another, is a small piece of no-man's land. If not for the conspicuous row of three large concrete cubes flanking one perimeter, this traffic triangle might remain indistinguishable from other slivers of similarly odd-shaped, leftover urban spaces found throughout the city. The cubic plinths are, in fact, the pedestals for three public sculptures by John Ahearn, sponsored by the Percent for Art program of the New York City Department of Cultural Affairs. Originally designed to serve as the bases for life-size bronze casts of Raymond Garcia (and his pit bull, Toby), Corey Mann, and Daleesha—all Ahearn's neighbors around Walton Avenue in the Bronx from the mid to late 1980s—the pedestals have remained empty, except for the accumulation of trash and graffiti, for about ten years. Since September 25, 1991, to be precise, when the artist himself had the sculptures removed only five days after their installation in response to protests by some residents and city officials who deemed them inappropriate for the site.[1]

In downtown Manhattan, at the juncture of Lafayette and Centre streets as they converge to become Nassau Street, there is another more or less triangular plot of public land, officially known as Foley Square. Framed by several formidable government buildings—United States Customs Court, Federal Office Building, New York County Court House, and United States Court House—the eastern perimeter of Foley Square faces Federal Plaza. This expansive plaza is populated with a set of large green mounds, perfect half-spheres that look like grass-covered igloos. Wrapping around the mounds is a series of serpentine benches, reiterating the circular form of the mounds and painted a bright apple green. Designed by well-known landscape architect Martha Schwartz, Federal Plaza today is a playful and decorative mix of street furniture and natural materials, a clever reworking of traditional design elements of urban parks. Seen from above, the plaza is an abstract composition in green, with yards of seating rippling through the space like highly contrived ribbons.

As many will recall, this last site, Federal Plaza, full of dynamic colors and user-friendly forms today, was once the site of a rancorous and vehement controversy concerning Richard Serra's steel sculpture *Tilted Arc.* Commissioned by the U.S. General Services Administration in 1979 and installed in 1981, the 12-foot-high, 120-foot-long sculpture was removed on March 15, 1989, after five years of public hearings, lawsuits, and plenty of media coverage concerning the legality and appropriateness of such an action. Now, a little over ten years later, the site has experienced a complete makeover. Martha Schwartz's redesign of Federal Plaza has erased all physical and historical traces of *Tilted Arc.*

So I begin here, with two "empty" sites of two "failed" public art works. The forlorn vacancy of the traffic triangle in the South Bronx and the specious pleasantness of Federal Plaza in downtown Manhattan bracket this chapter's consideration of the problematics of site specificity in the mainstream public art context.[2] One point to stress at the outset is the fact that even though site-specific modes of artistic practice emerged in the mid to late 1960s—roughly coinciding with the inception of the Art-in-Architecture Program of the General Services Administration (GSA) in 1963, the Art-in-Public-Places Program of the National Endowment for the Arts (NEA) in 1967, and numerous local and state Percent for Art programs throughout the 1960s—it was not until 1974 that concern to promote site-specific approaches to public art was first registered within the guidelines of these organizations, in particular the NEA. This lag is an initial indication that while the term "site specificity" might move fluidly through various cultures of artistic practice today—museums, galleries, alternative spaces, international biennials, public art programs—the history and implications of the term can be profoundly inconsistent from context to context. Thus, one task of this chapter is to chart the particular trajectory of site specificity within public art as a point of clarification. In particular, I will argue, the changing conceptualization of site specificity in the public art context indexes the changing criteria by which an art work's public relevance and its democratic sociopolitical ambitions have been imagined over the past three

◂ Martha Schwartz, Federal Plaza, New York, 1997–1998. (Photo by Seong H. Kwon.)

▸ View of South Bronx Sculpture Park site at Jerome and Gerard avenues and 169th Street (44th Precinct Police Station), c. 1992. (Photo by Nancy Owens.)

decades. Our story will concentrate on Ahearn's and Serra's cases to contemplate the meaningfulness of their respective "empty" sites, especially as they signal the limits and capacity of site specificity today.

Three distinct paradigms can be identified within the roughly 35-year history of the modern public art movement in the United States.[3] First, there is the art-in-public-places model exemplified by Alexander Calder's *La Grande Vitesse* in Grand Rapids, Michigan (1967), the first commission to be completed through the Art-in-Public-Places Program of the NEA. The second paradigm is the art-as-public-spaces approach, typified by design-oriented urban sculptures of Scott Burton, Siah Armajani, Mary Miss, Nancy Holt, and others, which function as street furniture, architectural constructions, or landscaped environments. Finally, there is the art-in-the-public-interest model, named as such by critic Arlene Raven and most cogently theorized by artist Suzanne Lacy under the heading of "new genre public art."[4] Select projects by artists such as John Malpede, Daniel Martinez, Hope Sandrow, Guillermo Gómez-Peña, Tim Rollins and K.O.S., and Peggy Diggs, among many others, are distinguished for foregrounding social issues and political activism, and/or for engaging "community" collaborations.[5]

Initially, from the mid 1960s to the mid 1970s, public art was dominated by the art-in-public-places paradigm—modernist abstract sculptures that were often enlarged replicas of works normally found in museums and galleries.[6] These art works were usually signature pieces from internationally established male artists (favored artists who received the most prominent commissions during this period include Isamu Noguchi, Henry Moore, and Alexander Calder). In and of themselves, they had no distinctive qualities to render them "public" except perhaps their size and scale.[7] What legitimated them as "public" art was quite simply their siting outdoors or in locations deemed to be public primarily because of their "openness" and unrestricted physical access—parks, university campuses, civic centers, entrance areas to federal buildings, plazas off city streets, parking lots, airports.

In the early 1970s, Henry Moore spoke of his relative indifference to the site, a position that is representative of many (though not all) artists working in the art-in-

Alexander Calder, ***La Grande Vitesse***, Grand Rapids, Michigan, 1967. (Photo courtesy of Grand Rapids City Hall.)

Isamu Noguchi, ***Red Cube***, Marine Midland Bank Plaza (now HSBC) at Broadway and Liberty Street, New York, 1968. (Photo by Miwon Kwon.)

public-places mode: "I don't like doing commissions in the sense that I go and look at a site and then think of something. Once I have been asked to consider a certain place where one of my sculptures might possibly be placed, I try to choose something suitable from what I've done or from what I'm about to do. But I don't sit down and try to create something especially for it."[8] Whether they were voluptuous abstractions of the human body in bronze or marble, colorful agglomerations of biomorphic shapes in steel, or fanciful plays on geometric forms in concrete, modernist public sculptures were conceived as autonomous works of art whose relationship to the site was at best incidental. Furthermore, just as the conditions of the site were considered irrelevant in the conception and production of a sculpture (because they functioned as distractions more than inspirations), so they needed to be suppressed at the point of reception if the sculpture was to speak forcefully to its viewers. Again in Moore's words: "To display sculpture to its best advantage outdoors, it must be set so that it relates to the sky rather than to trees, a house, people, or other aspects of its surroundings. Only the sky, miles away, allows us to contrast infinity with reality, and so we are able to discover the sculptor's inner scale without comparison."[9]

Thus the central issue preoccupying the artists of such public commissions (as well as their patrons or sponsors) was the proper placement of the discrete art work so as to best enhance and showcase its aesthetic qualities. The particular qualities of the site—in this case we are speaking primarily of the site as a physical, architectural entity—mattered only to the extent that they posed formal compositional challenges. For the architects involved, the art work was usually considered a beneficial visual supplement but finally an extraneous element to the integrity of a building or space. Contrarily, in many artists' views, the site remained a ground or pedestal upon which, or against which, the priority of the figure of the art work would be articulated. Such thinking was predicated on a strict separation between art and architecture (synonymous with the site) as two autonomous fields of practice, and it promoted complimentary visual contrast as the defining (formal) relationship between the two.

By bringing the "best" in contemporary art to a wider audience, by siting examples of it in public places, endeavors like the Art-in-Architecture Program of the GSA, the Art-in-Public-Places Program of the NEA, and the Percent for Art programs at local and state levels hoped to promote the aesthetic edification of the American public and to beautify the urban environment.[10] Public art works were meant to play a supplementary but crucial role in the amelioration of what were perceived to be the ill effects of the repetitive, monotonous, and functionalist style of modernist architecture. (The inclusion of artists within architectural design teams for the development of urban spaces in the art-as-public-spaces mode of practice, our second paradigm, continued to be predicated on the belief that with the artist's humanizing influence, the sense of alienation and disaffection engendered by the inhuman urban landscape of modernism could be rectified.[11] Which is to say, public art at this point was conceived as an antidote to modernist architecture and urban design.)

With such expectations at play, the art-in-public-places phenomenon had spread widely across the United States by the late 1970s.[12] Art historian Sam Hunter described the omnipresence of monumental abstract public sculptures in cities across the country around this time:

> In the seventies the triumph of the new public art was firmly secured. Almost any new corporate or municipal plaza worthy of its name deployed an obligatory large-scale sculpture, usually in a severely geometric, Minimalist style; or where more conservative tastes prevailed and funds were more generous, one might find instead a recumbent figure in bronze by Henry Moore or one of Jacques Lipchitz's mythological creatures. Today there is scarcely an American city of significant size boasting an urban-renewal program that lacks one or more large, readily identifiable modern sculptures to relieve the familiar stark vistas of concrete, steel, and glass.[13]

Despite the initial enthusiasm, as early as the mid 1970s the art-in-public-places approach began to be criticized for having very little to offer in the way of either aesthetic edification or urban beautification. Many critics and artists argued that autonomous signature-style art works sited in public places functioned more like extensions of the museum, advertising individual artists and their accomplishments (and by extension their patrons' status) rather than making any genuine gestures toward public engagement.[14] It was further argued that despite the physical accessibility, public art remained resolutely inaccessible insofar as the prevalent style of modernist abstraction remained indecipherable, uninteresting, and meaningless to a general audience. The art work's seeming indifference to the particular conditions of the site and/or its proximate audience was reciprocated by the public's indifference, even hostility, toward the foreignness of abstract art's visual language and toward its aloof and haughty physical presence in public places. Instead of a welcome reprieve in the flow of everyday urban life, public art seemed to be an unwanted imposition completely disengaged from it. Many critics, artists, and sponsors agreed that, at best, public art was a pleasant visual contrast to the rationalized regularity of its surroundings, providing a nice decorative effect. At worst, it was an empty trophy commemorating the powers and riches of the dominant class—a corporate bauble or architectural jewelry. And as the increasing private corporate sponsorship of public art became associated with the expansion of corporate real estate developments, pressures increased to rehabilitate the art-in-public-places programs.[15]

One of the key solutions to these interconnected problems of public art's public relations and its ineffectual influence on the urban environment was the adoption of site-specific principles for public art. Indeed, it was in reaction to the glut of ornamental "plop art"[16] and the monumental "object-off-the-pedestal" paradigm that, for instance, the NEA changed its guidelines in 1974 to stipulate, even if somewhat vaguely, that public art works needed to be "appropriate to the immediate site."[17] Whereas the program's initial 1965 goals had been to support individual artists of exceptional talent and demonstrated ability and to provide the public with opportunities to experience the best of American contemporary art, new mandates at all levels of public art sponsorship and funding now stipulated that the specificities of the site should influence, if not determine, the final artistic outcome.[18] Thus, despite the numerous pragmatic and bureaucratic difficulties in commissioning new art works (certainly it is simpler to purchase existing ones), the support for site-specific approaches to public art, favoring the creation of unique and unrepeatable aesthetic responses tailored to specific locations within a city, became fairly quickly institutionalized.[19] In the minds of those intimately engaged with the public art industry at the time, including artists, administrators, and critics, establishing a direct formal link between the material configuration of the art work and the existing physical conditions of the site—instead of emphasizing their disconnection or autonomy—seemed like a very good idea. Such an approach was advocated as an important step toward making art works more accessible and socially responsible, that is, more public.

Interestingly, the issue of modernist abstract art's interpretive (in)accessibility was defined as a spatial problem by many in the public art field in the late 1970s and early 1980s. For example, Janet Kardon, the curator of the 1980 exhibition "Urban Encounters: Art Architecture Audience," claimed in her catalogue essay:

> The way the abstract art work relates to the space of the passer-by is one key to the negative reception that has become a kind of certificate of merit among modern artists. . . . It unsettles perceptions and does not reassure the viewer with an easily shared idea or subject. . . . Entry [into a work] is facilitated when the public perceives the work as performing some useful task, whether it is simply that of shade and seating, or something even remotely associated with the sense of leisure. To be guided through space in a way that rewards the passer-by is of prime value to the public.[20]

A cocontributor to the same exhibition catalogue, Nancy Foote, took the notion of "entry" more literally, going so far as to say that only site-specific works that "invite the audience in," both physically and iconographically, reveal a public commitment.[21] Similarly, critics Kate Linker and Lawrence Alloway believed that art that becomes integrated with the physical site offers the greatest sustainability as well as potential for fluid communication and interaction with a general nonart audience. According to Linker, "To the absence of a shared iconography, it suggests the shareable presence of space. . . . Just as use insures relevance, so the appeal to space as a social experience, communal scope, individual response, may insure a larger measure of support."[22] In these critics' writings of the early 1980s, physical access or entry *into* an art work is imagined to be equivalent to hermeneutic access for the viewer.

The various agencies' programmatic enforcement of a continuity between the art work and its site, however, was predicated on a kind of architectural determinism endemic to most urban beautification efforts. Implicit in such thinking was the belief in an unmediated causal relationship between the aesthetic quality of the built environment and the quality of social conditions it supported. Consequently, the type of site specificity stipulated by the NEA, GSA, and other public art agencies was directed toward spatial integration and harmonious design.[23] By now, artists were asked not only to focus on the conditions of the built environment but to contribute toward the design of unified and coherent urban spaces. This is partly why, by the end of the 1970s, the NEA endorsed a "wide range of possibilities for art in public situations"—"any permanent media, including earthworks, environmental art, and non-traditional media, such as artificial lighting."[24] The aim was not only to accommodate the changing artistic trends of the period but to align public art more with the production of public amenities and site-oriented projects. What this amounted to in essence was a mandate for public art to be more like architecture and environmental design.

This integrationist goal was further strengthened when the NEA guidelines were modified once again in 1982, with the Visual Art and Design programs of the NEA officially combining their efforts to encourage the collaboration of visual artists and design professionals. Public art would no longer be just an autonomous sculpture but would be in some kind of meaningful dialogue with, maybe even coincident with, the surrounding architecture and/or landscape. This approach to site-specific public art was readily adopted by a group of artists, including Athena Tacha, Ned Smyth, Andrea Blum, Siah Armajani, Elyn Zimmerman, and Scott Bur-

Nancy Holt, ***Dark Star Park***, Rosslyn, Virginia, 1979–1984. (© Nancy Holt/VAGA, New York.)

ton. Unsatisfied with the decorative function of public art in the earlier model of art-in-public-places, and excited by the opportunity to pursue their work outside the confines of museums and galleries at an unprecedented scale and complexity (and with the expectation of addressing a much larger and broader audience), many artists were eager to accept, or at least test, the design team directive. Ideally, they would now share responsibilities on equal footing with architects and urban planners in making design decisions about public spaces.[25]

Adopted in the process was a functionalist ethos that prioritized public art's use value over its aesthetic value, or measured its aesthetic value in terms of use value. This shift, predicated on the desire of many artists and public art agencies to reconcile the division between art and utility—in order to render public art more accessible, accountable, and relevant to the public—conflated the art work's use value, narrowly defined in relation to simple physical needs (such as seating and shading), with social responsibility. As Rosalyn Deutsche has argued, physical utility was reductively and broadly equated with social benefit with this kind of art, and "social activity [was] constricted to narrow problem solving so that the provision of useful objects automatically collapsed into a social good."[26]

This collapse was explicit in much public art of the 1980s that followed the collaborative design team model, and was especially notable in the work and words of Scott Burton and his supporters.[27] Many artists and critics alike seemed to think that the more an art work disappeared into the site, either by appropriating urban street furniture (benches and tables, street lamps, manhole covers, fencing) or by mimicking familiar architectural elements (gateways, columns, floors, walls, stairways, bridges, urban plazas, lobbies, parks), the greater its social value would be. During the same time, other artists such as Les Levine, Krzysztof Wodiczko, Group Material, Guerrilla Girls, and Dennis Adams, among many others, were exploring alternative strategies of adopting existing urban forms as sites of artistic intervention. But their appropriation of different modes of public address, particularly those of media and advertising, including billboards, newspapers, and television, usually for the purposes of deconstructing or redirecting their familiar function, did not garner the same kind of official support within the public art industry until later in

◂ Lobby of the Wiesner Arts and Media Building at MIT, Cambridge, Massachusetts, by I. M. Pei & Partners. Bench and railing by Scott Burton, color pattern design on interior walls by Kenneth Noland, exterior plaza paving design by Richard Fleischner, all 1985. (© Steve Rosenthal; courtesy I. M. Pei & Partners.)

▸ Richard Serra, ***Tilted Arc***, Federal Plaza, New York, 1981–1989. (Photo by Ann Chauvet; © Richard Serra/Artists Rights Society (ARS), New York.)

the decade.[28] In the meantime, the more an art work abandoned its distinctive look of "art" to seamlessly assimilate to the site, as defined by the conventions of architecture and urban design, the more it was hailed as a progressive artistic gesture.

It is against this prevailing definition of site specificity—one of unified and useful urban design, imagined as a model of social harmony and unity—that Richard Serra proposed a counterdefinition with his massive, wall-like steel sculpture *Tilted Arc.* As early as 1980, several years before he was forced to consolidate his thoughts on site specificity to defend his sculpture for the Federal Plaza site, he explicitly rejected the then widespread tendency of public sculpture to accommodate architectural design. He declared,

> There seems to be in this country [United States] right now, especially in sculpture, a tendency to make work which attends to architecture. I am not interested in work which is structurally ambiguous, or in sculpture which satisfies urban design principles. I have always found that to be not only an aspect of mannerism but a need to reinforce a status quo of existing aesthetics. . . . I am interested in sculpture which is non-utilitarian, non-functional . . . any use is a misuse.[29]

Considering such an aggressive statement in light of the GSA's guidelines of the same period—"Such [public art] works are intended to be an integral part of the total architectural design and enhance the building's environment for the occupants and the general public"[30]—it may seem a wonder that Serra was even considered for the Federal Plaza commission. But the incongruity only reminds us of the discrepancy at the heart of the selection process at this time: that is, the discrepancy between the values of the committee of art experts, who obviously responded to Serra's already established international reputation as an artist, and the criteria guiding the administrators of the GSA, who deferred to the experts on issues of artistic merit.

In any case, as critics Rosalyn Deutsche and Douglas Crimp have separately affirmed, Serra indeed proposed an interruptive and interventionist model of site specificity, quite explicitly opposed to an integrationist or assimilative one.[31] Deutsche has argued that public art discourse's use of the term site specificity to connote the creation of harmonious spatial totalities is close to a "terminological abuse," insofar as site-specific art emerged from "the imperative to interrupt, rather than secure, the seeming coherence and closure of those spaces [of the art work's display]."[32] In her view, *Tilted Arc* reasserted the critical basis of site specificity, countering its neutralization in the public art of the 1980s. In doing so, it revealed the incompatibility of site specificity with the kind of objectives held by the GSA.

My concern here, however, is not so much to establish the right definition of site specificity as to examine the ways in which competing definitions emerge and operate in the public art field, and to assess their varied artistic, social, and political implications and consequences. The terms of Serra's "critical" or "political" site specificity,[33] in fact, remain more ambiguous than one might expect. This is in large part due to the emphasis placed on permanence as a fundamental attribute of site specificity during the *Tilted Arc* controversy. Serra himself mounted his argument against the "relocation" of his sculpture on the premise that, first and foremost, site-specific art has an inviolable physical tie to its site. Hence, to remove the work is to destroy the work. He insisted throughout and after the controversy that

> *Tilted Arc* was conceived from the start as a site-specific sculpture and was not meant to be "site-adjusted" or . . . "relocated." Site-specific works deal with the environmental components of given places. The scale, size, and location of site-specific works are determined by the topography of the site, whether it be urban or landscape or architectural enclosure. The works become part of the site and restructure both conceptually and perceptually the organization of the site.[34]

While the insistence on permanence during the court hearings might have had some legal exigency, the priority given to the issue has obscured certain other aspects of *Tilted Arc*'s site specificity.[35] For instance, Serra does seem to prioritize the physical relationship between the art work and site in comments like the following from the same article: "The specificity of site-oriented works means that they are conceived for, dependent upon, and inseparable from their locations. The scale, the size, and the placement of sculptural elements result from an analysis of the particular environmental components of a given context."[36] But he goes on to say that "the preliminary analysis of a given site takes into consideration not only formal but also social and political characteristics of the site. Site-specific works invariably manifest a judgment about the larger social and political context of which they are a part."[37]

In other words, the site is imagined as a social and political construct as well as a physical one. More importantly, Serra envisions not a relationship of smooth continuity between the art work and its site but an antagonistic one in which the art work performs a proactive interrogation—"manifest[s] a judgment" (presumably negative)—about the site's sociopolitical conditions. Indeed, rather than fulfilling an ameliorative function in relation to the site, *Tilted Arc* aggressively cut across and divided it. (No seating, shading, or other physical accommodations here.) In doing so, as proponents of the sculpture have pointed out, *Tilted Arc* literalized the social divisions, exclusions, and fragmentation that manicured and aesthetically tamed public spaces generally disguise. In destroying the illusion of Federal Plaza as a coherent spatial totality, Serra underscored its already dysfunctional status as a public space.

According to Serra, it is only in working against the given site in this way that art can resist cooptation.

> Works which are built within the contextual frame of governmental, corporate, educational, and religious institutions run the risk of being read as tokens of those institutions. . . . Every context has its frame and its ideological overtones. It is a matter of degree. But there are sites where it is obvious that an art work is being subordinated to / accommodated to / adapted to / subservient to / useful to. . . . In

> such cases it is necessary to work in opposition to the constraints of the context so that the work cannot be read as an affirmation of questionable ideologies and political power. I am not interested in art as affirmation or complicity.[38]

Thus, in Serra's practice, site specificity is constituted as a precise *discomposure* between the art work and its site. And this discomposure—which is antithetical both to the notion of art's and architecture's complementary juxtaposition, as in the art-in-public-places model, and to that of their seamless continuity, as in the art-as-public-spaces model—is intended to bring into relief the repressed social contradictions that underlie public spaces, like Federal Plaza, rendering them perceptible, thus knowable, to the viewing subjects of the sculpture.

It is important to point out at this juncture that, in Serra's case, this critical function of site-specific art is directly tied to a critique of the medium-specific concerns of modernist art.[39] As Serra explained, "Unlike modernist works that give the illusion of being autonomous from their surroundings, and which function critically only in relation to the language of their own medium, site-specific works emphasize the comparison between two separate languages and can therefore use the language of one to criticize the language of the other."[40] So that in addition to working against the physical and sociopolitical conditions of the site, the art work simultaneously addresses the site itself as another *medium,* an "other language." Put a little differently, working against the site coincides with working against the modernist illusion of artistic autonomy. In Serra's case, the "other" to his own language of sculpture is architecture. And architecture, in turn, serves as the material manifestation of "questionable ideologies and political power," which Serra is interested in exposing and subverting. So that in the end, working site-specifically means working against architecture.[41]

This is not to say, however, that this "working against" is a straightforward opposition. Note that Serra never speaks, for instance, of merging sculpture and architecture into some new hybrid form to obliterate their categorical distinctions (as so many contemporary artists are prone to do today in the name of radicalizing

Richard Serra, ***Tilted Arc***, Federal Plaza, New York, 1981–1989. (© Richard Serra/Artists Rights Society (ARS), New York; courtesy Leo Castelli Gallery, New York.)

artistic practice). In fact, the question of sculpture has remained central in his practice over thirty years—not despite but because of the extent to which he has pressured sculpture to the brink of dissolution. As Hal Foster has written recently, "with Serra sculpture becomes its deconstruction, its making becomes its unmaking. . . . To deconstruct sculpture is to serve its 'internal necessity,' to extend sculpture in relation to process, embodiment, and site is to remain within it."[42] To some readers, this imperative of serving an "internal necessity" may sound like an ontological quest, if not a modernist one, contrary to Serra's critique of medium specificity. But according to Foster, the paradoxical principle of making sculpture through its unmaking distinguishes a "*medium-differential*" investigation of the category of "sculpture" from a medium-specific one. It acknowledges that sculpture is no longer established in advance or known in certainty, but "must be forever proposed, tested, reworked, and proposed again."[43] Which is to reiterate the point that Serra's site specificity addresses not only the particular physical, social, and political attributes of a place; it is at the same time engaged in an *art*-specific inquiry or critique (or perhaps art discourse is itself a site), proposing, testing, reworking, and proposing again what sculpture might be. Indeed, for Serra, site specificity has been both a means to move beyond sculpture and simultaneously a "medium"[44] through which to serve its "internal necessity."

To the opponents of *Tilted Arc* in the mid 1980s, however, the nuances of such aesthetic concerns did not matter much. In fact, supportive testimonies to the importance of this "great work of art," or advocating the right of the artist to pursue free expression without governmental interference or censorship, were countered by resentful commentaries of varying animosity.[45] Some regarded the sculpture as plain, ugly, and brutal, without any artistic merit whatsoever. Some found its presence on the plaza physically and psychologically oppressive. Few waxed nostalgic over the past uses of a (falsely remembered) vitally active public plaza (an "oasis of respite and relaxation"),[46] accusing *Tilted Arc* of destroying this past, of violating a public amenity.[47] A security expert even testified on the ways in which the sculpture created an impediment to surveillance, encouraging loitering, graffiti, and possible terrorist bomb attacks.

Complaints of this type were presented as the voices of "the people" during the 1985 hearings, and the government officials in charge of the proceedings presumed to speak for the public—on behalf of its needs and interests—in their call for the removal of the sculpture. They characterized *Tilted Arc* as an arrogant and highly inappropriate assertion of a private self on public grounds. The sculpture was viewed, in other words, as another kind of plop art. At the same time, despite the artist's ardent efforts to maintain a certain "uselessness" for his sculpture (or actually because of this), *Tilted Arc* was instrumentalized by its opponents as a symbol of the overbearing imposition of the federal government (the sponsor of the sculpture) in the lives of "ordinary" citizens and "their" spaces. In the end, the removal of *Tilted Arc* was characterized as tantamount to the reclaiming of public space by the "community"—narrowly defined as those living or working in the immediate neighborhoods around Federal Plaza.

But as Rosalyn Deutsche has argued, the meaning of key words deployed during this conflict, such as "use," "public," "public use," and "community," were presumed to be self-evident, based on "common sense." Even those of the left who supported *Tilted Arc* did not contest in any effective way the essential and universalizing definitions of these terms—and their ideological uses in the very name of neutrality and objectivity—as they framed the entire debate.[48] In Deutsche's view, the opportunity was regrettably missed, both during the hearings and after (especially with the publication of the documents pertaining to the controversy), to challenge the authoritarian uses of these terms in the name of "the people," a tendency that is not exclusive to right-wing politicians but prevalent in left-informed public art discourse as well. She has also reminded us that the final decision to remove *Tilted Arc* was not a decision against public art in general, for city governments, corporations, and real estate developers have long understood the benefits of public art in mobilizing support for redevelopment and gentrification of urban spaces. Instead, according to Deutsche, *Tilted Arc*'s removal was a discrediting of a particular model of public art—or a particular model of site specificity, as I would insist—one without obvious utilitarian payoffs, one that critically questions rather than promotes the fantasies of public space as a unified totality without conflicts or difference.

While similarly intense debates have accompanied the unveiling of numerous public art works of the past,[49] the *Tilted Arc* incident made most clear that public art is not simply a matter of giving "public access to the best art of our times outside museum walls."[50] In fact, much more was riding on the *Tilted Arc* case than the fate of a single art work. Unlike prior public art disputes, this controversy, as one of the most high-profile battlegrounds for the broad-based "culture wars" of the late 1980s, put to the test the very life of public funding for the arts in the United States.[51] This is why critics like Deutsche have insisted that conflicts such as the one over *Tilted Arc* reveal the extent to which public art discourse functions as a site of political struggle over the meaning of democracy.[52]

Perhaps recognizing the political stakes more self-consciously than ever, public art practitioners and administrators engaged in considerable soul-searching following the *Tilted Arc* debate, reexamining the fundamental questions of public art's goals and procedures. For even if the various testimonies against *Tilted Arc* could be dismissed as uninformed populist thinking, or as motivated by corrupt reactionary politics, or as simply wrong-headed, some complaints had to be taken seriously for at least two reasons. First, it was a matter of survival. In the tide of neoconservative Republicanism during the 1980s, with the attack on governmental funding for the arts (the NEA in particular) reaching a hysterical pitch by 1989, public art programs had to strategically rearticulate their goals and methods in order to avoid the prospect of annihilation or complete privatization (which might amount to the same thing). Secondly, even those public art professionals most sympathetic to Serra's cause had to recognize that there was a bit of truth in some of the criticism. For the point of contestation that mattered most was not so much the artistic merit of Serra's sculpture but the exclusionary (and some did say elitist) commissioning procedures of public art agencies like the GSA and the NEA. Congressman Theodore Weiss testified against *Tilted Arc* during the hearings in these terms:

> *Tilted Arc* was imposed upon this neighborhood without discussion, without prior consultation, without any of the customary dialogue that one expects between government and its people. The National Endowment for the Arts panel of three selected the artist and a three person group from the General Services Administration in Washington, D.C., approved the design. No one else—not from the community or its representatives, not the architects, not even the Regional Administrators—was ever consulted. These panels, no matter how expert or how well-intentioned, are not so omnipotent or infallible in their judgments that they cannot be challenged or improved upon.[53]

Arguably, the seeds of this argument—that *Tilted Arc* was absolutely inappropriate to the site because the top-down decision-making process, dictated by small review panels of art experts and bureaucrats, did not involve the members of the local community—has had the most far-reaching impact on the direction of the public art discourse of the 1990s. Even before the blowup over *Tilted Arc,* some public artists and administrators had recognized that the site of a public art work had to be imagined beyond its physical attributes. Ideally, the work should engage the site socially, instigating "community involvement." But initially, this seems to have been motivated primarily by the need to forestall potentially hostile reception of certain public art works. In 1979, for example, when the NEA requested that its grant recipients provide "methods to insure an informed community response to the project,"[54] the community was still conceived as an inadequately prepared audience. The community, in other words, needed to be engaged in order to soften them to the "best art of our time," to educate them in its proper interpretation and appreciation (not unlike the way audience groups are commonly treated in museums).[55]

But by the late 1980s, and certainly by the time of *Tilted Arc*'s removal, "community involvement" meant more. At the bureaucratic level, it meant the expanded inclusion of nonart community representatives in the selection panels and review committees of public art commissions. More significantly, it suggested a dialogue between the artist and his/her immediate audience, with the possibility of community participation, even collaboration, in the making of the art work. For many artists and administrators with long-standing commitments to community-based practices since the 1960s, or what Suzanne Lacy has retroactively called "new genre public art," an intensive engagement with the people of the site, involving direct communication and interaction over an extended period of time, had been a well-established tenet of socially responsible and ethically sound public art. That such a model of public art was marginalized, even denigrated, by the official public art establishment for over three decades[56] must have made the *Tilted Arc* incident a point of profound ambivalence for many community-oriented practitioners. Even though some public artists and administrators were traumatized by the *Tilted Arc* controversy and its outcome,[57] the sculpture's removal from Federal Plaza, when viewed as a triumphal rejection of "high art" by "the people," also signaled an implicit validation of the community-oriented approach to public art.

The discursive emergence of new genre public art in 1989, in fact, coincides with the removal of *Tilted Arc*,[58] and Lacy subsequently refers to the *Tilted Arc* case as an occasion "when office workers' demands to remove the sculpture from the site in a civic plaza led to calls for greater public accountability by artists."[59] The controversy is cast as an exemplary instance of "the conventions of artistic expression . . . com[ing] into conflict with public opinion," with public opinion winning.[60] Of course, such a reading of the *Tilted Arc* incident unquestioningly accepts the terms of the debate as defined by the sculpture's opponents. It challenges instead Serra's critique of conventions of artistic expression as itself conventional. In the view of many public artists and administrators, Serra did little to complicate, for instance, the security of individual authorship; in fact, during the hearings, he seemed to argue for its inviolability against the wishes of "the public." Moreover, they saw that Serra's artistic pursuit, no matter how complex and genuine its critical engagement with the site and its sociopolitical issues, was still driven primarily by art-specific concerns that had little bearing on the lives of the people who constitute the actual, rather than abstract or metaphorical, reality of the site. Therefore, the radicalizing effects of his art work remained narrowly confined to art discourse only, legible to a limited, art-educated audience, appreciated most notably by a small group of influential voices professionally ensconced in art criticism, art history, and the museum world.

Indeed, Lacy implicates Serra in such statements as: "Although the move to exhibit art in public places was a progressive one, the majority of artists accommodated themselves to the established museum system, continuing to focus their attention on art critics and museum-going connoisseurs."[61] Whereas numerous art experts confirmed the radicality of *Tilted Arc*'s aesthetic and social critique, then, those aligned with community-based public art did not find the work radical enough.[62] Insofar as Serra never opens up the creative process to a collaboration or dialogue with the community (he has in fact disdained the need for art to please its audience as well as its sponsors), and insofar as the sculpture's particular form of criticality coalesces as Serra's "signature," his work is held to have no impact on the hermetic boundaries of the art world and its institutionalized hierarchies of value. From this point of view, works like *Tilted Arc* are an unwanted encroachment of art world values into the spaces of everyday life and people, and an individual's artistic concerns are, by definition, antithetical to a socially progressive way of thinking. In this way, a peculiar alignment developed between the "authoritarian populism"[63] of the right and the community advocacy of the new genre public art type on the left. Both rejected a certain kind of critical art in the name of "the people."[64]

Certainly by the spring of 1986, little over a year after the hearings on *Tilted Arc*, the directive to involve the community in the public art process was being taken more seriously in New York City and elsewhere, with the NEA taking the lead in 1983 with instructions to include "plans for community involvement, preparation, and dialogue."[65] So that when it came to choosing an artist for the Percent for Art commission at the 44th Precinct police station in the South Bronx, John Ahearn was an "obvious choice" for the selection panel, which now included several nonart representatives.[66] According to Tom Finklepearl, former Director of New York City's Percent for Art program, Ahearn "was an obvious choice because he lived close to the station, enjoyed a good critical reputation, and had already spent many years interacting with the community. . . . He was well acquainted with the specific nature of the community within which the commission was sited, and worked in a figurative style that is considered accessible."[67] In other words, Ahearn represented the antithesis of Serra; or in Finklepearl's words, "Ahearn fit the mold for the 'post-Serra' artist perfectly."[68]

Certainly the differences between the two artists are striking. Serra came into prominence in the late 1960s, with the emergence of postminimalism and process art in particular, as part of the American neo-avant-garde generation. He is distinguished by art historians and art institutions worldwide as one of the most important sculptors of the twentieth century. Ahearn found an audience in the very late 1970s and early 1980s during the rise of the alternative art scenes in the East Village and the Bronx. He remains biographically linked to the South Bronx and is modestly self-described as an "itinerant portrait painter."[69]

The most significant difference relevant to our discussion, however, is the fact that whereas Serra intended an aggressively interruptive function for his sculpture on Federal Plaza, Ahearn sought an assimilative one for his at Jerome Avenue. Ahearn imagined a continuity rather than a rupture between his sculptures and the social life of the neighborhood where the works were to be displayed and to which they "belonged." This is not to say that he did not recognize the potential for conflict with, specifically, the 44th Precinct police officers. After all, few of them had hoped for an art work depicting the local police presence as congenial and welcomed. But Ahearn's acknowledgment of the police as a key audience group only deepened his commitment to creating an accurate and humane representation of the site's reality as he knew it. He wanted to counter the prevalent negative stereotypes of the Bronx (harbored by the police in particular and promoted by the mass media) as a place of urban decay and economic devastation, as a dangerous and violent place infested with drug dealers, criminals, prostitutes, gangs, and disease.[70] Instead, he wanted his work to embody what he called the "South Bronx attitude"[71]—resilient, proud, unpretentious, and "real." In attempting to capture the authenticity of the site in this way, Ahearn in effect intended a different model of site specificity, a community-based realism that countered the example of Serra's *Tilted Arc,* which itself was a counterposition to the art-as-public-spaces model of public art.

John Ahearn, view of South Bronx Sculpture Park (at 44th Precinct Police Station), with sculptures of Raymond and Tobey, Daleesha, and Corey, on day of installation, 1991. (© Ari Marcopoulos; courtesy Alexander and Bonin Gallery, New York.)

John Ahearn and Rigoberto Torres, casting Hazel Santiago at a Walton Avenue block party, Bronx, New York, September 3, 1985. (Photo by Ivan Dalla Tana; courtesy Alexander and Bonin Gallery, New York.)

Clearly, Ahearn understood that to produce a mural or any other architectural embellishment for the new police station, as was suggested to him at an early stage of the commission, would be a terrible mistake.[72] In fact, it was his decision, and not that of the Department of Cultural Affairs or the Department of General Services (DGS), to work with the dead space of the traffic triangle facing the station precisely in order to *confront* the station rather than be part of it. At some level, he had internalized Serra's earlier insight that "works which are built within the contextual frame of governmental, corporate, educational, and religious institutions run the risk of being read as tokens of those institutions."[73] But while Ahearn resisted making his art work a token of various institutions of power, privilege, and authority—the police, the Department of Cultural Affairs, the art world—he actively sought ways to submit the work to, to put it in service of, the largely African American and Puerto Rican community of his neighborhood. Ahearn attempted to resist the function of site-specific public art to support the ideologies and political power of dominant social groups, affirming instead his allegiance to those groups disempowered and marginalized by these ideologies and power.

The artist's identification with the local community of blacks and Latinos developed more or less organically over a decade. Since 1980 Ahearn had been living on Walton Avenue between 171st and 172nd streets, just a few blocks from the traffic triangle. Even as his artistic career ascended through the decade, with exhibitions in "legitimate" art world venues, he maintained the center of his art and life there in a sixth-floor slum apartment. He produced most of his art directly on the street: he regularly set up shop on the sidewalk outside his studio, casting portraits of neighborhood residents, including many children and teenagers, who often contributed comments on how they would like to be represented. By making two copies of every portrait, one for him to keep and the other to be taken home by the sitter, Ahearn devised a very specific economy of intimate exchange and local distribution for his art. Even as he exhibited and sold some of the portraits as fine art through his SoHo gallery, he also made sure that they became part of the everyday culture of his neighborhood, proudly displayed by individuals in their living rooms, bedrooms, kitchens, and dining rooms.

In many street casting sessions, he collaborated with Rigoberto (Robert) Torres,[74] an artist from the neighborhood whom Ahearn had met in 1979 after an exhibition of his relief sculptures at Fashion Moda, an alternative gallery space that had opened a year before on Third Avenue and 149th Street.[75] Between 1981 and 1985, Torres and Ahearn together produced four very popular sculptural murals for the sides of tenement buildings—*We Are Family, Life on Dawson Street, Double Dutch,* and *Back to School*—that picture quotidian aspects of life in the neighborhood. Even though some art critics judged these wall works and other cast pieces to be overly sentimental, and even though the artist himself worried at times that they were too much like folk art, as long as the work made his neighbors "happy," Ahearn thought of them as achieving more meaningful and difficult goals than what is usually expected of an art work. In his words, the "discipline of 'happy' is just as important as the discipline of 'strong' or 'tough,'" and the cast sculptures made to please a neighbor are "purer than something with too much of myself in it, something individual."[76]

Through sustained years of intimate collaborative exchanges and in situ interactions, Ahearn naturally came to see himself as integral to the culture of the neighborhood (as many others did). As relayed by Jane Kramer, the author of a lengthy *New Yorker* article on this South Bronx project (later published as a book), the artist believed that with Robert Torres he was "part of what was happening in the Bronx, part of the integrity of the neighborhood, and solidly at home."[77] Because of this, the artist saw the site on Jerome Avenue not so much as an abstract formal entity but as an extension of the community, of which he himself was a part. Ahearn's personal history and sense of identity was directly tied to the location. And this continuity is what made him such an "obvious choice" for the Department of Cultural Affairs as well as other city agencies and committees, including the Bronx Community Board Four, which reviewed the maquettes for the project in 1990 and gave its "community" approval without hesitation.

Yet the attacks against Ahearn and the sculptures that finally led to their removal were exactly on the grounds that neither belonged to the "community," that the sculptures were inappropriate for the site. At one end were officials from the

John Ahearn and Rigoberto Torres, ***Back to School***, installed at Walton Avenue and 172nd Street, Bronx, New York, 1985. (Photo by Ivan Dalla Tana; courtesy Alexander and Bonin Gallery, New York.)

Department of General Services who were overseeing the station building project as a whole. Arthur Symes, a black architect, who had newly taken on the role of assistant commissioner in charge of design and construction management, and Claudette LaMelle, a black administrator and executive assistant to the commissioner of the DGS, felt that regardless of his outstanding reputation as an artist and his track record living and working in the South Bronx, Ahearn, as a white man, could never understand the experience of the African American "community." Thus he had no capacity to represent it accurately for or in the Bronx. They charged that, in fact, the sculptures were racist.[78] On the other end were the complaints of a small group of residents from an apartment building at the Jerome Avenue traffic triangle, who found the sculptures an absolute misrepresentation of *their* community. They accused Ahearn of glorifying illegitimate members of the community, or "roof people," according to Mrs. Salgado, the most vocal opponent of the sculptures. In their eyes, Ahearn had literally and symbolically elevated the derelict, criminal, and delinquent elements of the community. They argued that in essence Ahearn promoted the outsider's view of the Bronx with negative stereotypes (the two male figures in particular), and that with these sculptures he affirmed the police's distorted perceptions of the community, exacerbating the already tense relations with them.

In Ahearn's view, of course, the three sculptures—of Daleesha, a young black teenage girl on roller skates; Corey, a large shirtless black man leaning over a boom box, holding a basketball; and Raymond, a slender Puerto Rican man in a hooded sweatshirt, squatting next to his pit bull—represented a certain truth about the neighborhood. Perhaps not a truth that everyone would want to embrace, but an indigenous truth nonetheless. He found Daleesha, Corey, and Raymond (whom he knew personally, the last two as friends even) appropriate subjects to commemorate as survivors of the mean streets. He wanted to capture their humanity and make its beauty visible to the policemen at the 44th Precinct as well as to the neighbors, in the hope of ameliorating the sense of distrust and hostility between them. As Kramer notes, Ahearn "wanted the police to acknowledge them, and he wanted the neighbors, seeing them cast in bronze and up on pedestals, to stop and think about who they were. . . . John wanted them to stand in something of the same relation to the precinct policemen that they do to him and the neighbors. They may be trouble, but they are human, and they are there."[79] Despite Ahearn's earnest intentions, however, the sculptures provoked anger rather than empathy among many neighbors.[80] In fact, the sculptures were seen as an insult to the community in that they depicted people most neighbors found menacing, fearsome, and threatening—the kind of people that they would want police protection *from.* As Angela Salgado, Mrs. Salgado's daughter, put it, it was people like Corey and Raymond that made "the difference between a working-class neighborhood and a ghetto." As such, she also charged the sculptures with being "totems of racism."[81]

Within the context of early 1990s multiculturalist identity politics and political correctness debates (do-good community-based public art is itself a symptom of this period), such accusations were perhaps too tricky to counter. Ahearn did not even attempt arguing against them in any systematic or sustained way. Initially he tried speaking to the few detractors who gathered at the site, especially Mrs. Salgado. He approached her respectfully to have a dialogue—to introduce himself and his work, and to listen to her. He even repainted Raymond's face the morning after installation to have him appear less menacing, less "Halloween," so that Mrs. Salgado might see "the other Raymond," "beautiful *and* heavy."[82] But he could not dissuade her from seeing his bronzes as evil and ugly, a "slap in the community's face." In the end, Mrs. Salgado's objections and his inability to convince her became a measure of the work's failure for Ahearn.

> To the art world, my bronzes were serious, ironic. They had oomph, they were strong. They were an "artist's" pieces, and they looked good at the site, but I thought that day, "They'll never look like this again." I knew that soon they'd look terrible. Bad. Uglier than Mrs. Salgado said. So I said, "Fuck 'em, the art world!" It's not my job to be fighting these conservative progressive people—people like Mrs. Salgado. I respect these people. It's not my job to be the punk artist in the neighborhood—like, there's a lot going on in my artistic life besides this installation. There's my concept of casts in people's

homes—the execution may be shoddy, but to me those casts are more valuable than a bronze, or a better piece in a collector's home, and if I've misread my people it means I've misread myself and my concept. . . . What I felt was, I had a choice. . . . Either I was going to be on Mrs. Salgado's side or I was going to be her enemy. I refused that.[83]

Acknowledging that he had miscalculated the situation, he removed the sculptures at his own expense five days after their installation. Thus a project that began as one made with, of, and for the community, by an artist presumed to be an integral part of that community and approved by a committee of community leaders, was in the end disowned by the community. In a recent interview, Ahearn has remarked on the nature of the site itself as part of the problem:

In previous times when we installed the wall murals a supportive community would all come out in strength to view their friends being hoisted up on the wall. It was a family situation. Whereas the installation of the bronzes was a little bit removed from the neighborhood that I lived in, even though it was only four blocks away. It was just far enough away that it only got a stray group of onlookers that I recognized. Unlike earlier days, the few friends of mine from downtown that showed up outnumbered the local community, which made me a bit uneasy. There was a disquiet to the day. Already as the pieces were unveiled, there were arguments at the site as to the purpose of the work. That had never happened with the murals. In earlier times, the murals were seen as a private thing within the community, but this was instantly understood to be of a citywide, public nature. This was perceived as a city site. . . . People could tell the difference. People felt that this had to do with the city, not with their community.[84]

Of course, the ambiguity of the term "community" is one of the central issues here. At any one time, depending on who is speaking, the community could be the people around a few buildings on Walton Avenue, where Ahearn, Daleesha, Corey, and Raymond are familiar faces; or it could be the group of people living several blocks away on Jerome Avenue, where Ahearn, Daleesha, Corey, and Raymond are viewed as outsiders; or it could be constituencies delineated by the outlines of voting districts; or it might conjure "the Bronx" as an almost mythical place; or then again, it may not be tied to a geographical area at all but defined instead in terms of a shared historical and racial background, as was the case with the administrators at the DGS in their presumption of a singular African American community.

In Ahearn's case, it is relatively easy to trace these various expectations at work, both within the artist's practice and outside it. The rationale behind the selection of him for the South Bronx commission, as cited earlier, is a case in point. But the later contestation over Ahearn's capacity and right to represent the community, and the accompanying protests against the choice of Daleesha, Corey, and Raymond as representative of the community, are also based on such expectations. That is, while there may be disagreements among different groups over the specifics, the dominant principle or operative basis of community-based site specificity is the presumption of a unity of identity between the artist and the community, and between the community and the art work. Indeed, the commonality of this belief is the *source* of the disagreements, as we have seen in Ahearn's case.

The ambiguity of the term "community," which is consistent with the discursive slippage around "audience,"[85] "site," and "public," is itself a distinctive trait of community-based public art discourse. As such, the claims made of and for the "community" by artists, curators, administrators, critics, and various audience groups demand extensive critical analysis. To contribute to that end, I will delineate here what seems to be the underlying logic of community-based site specificity as exemplified by Ahearn's South Bronx project, some aspects of which have been already outlined in contrast to the site specificity of Richard Serra's *Tilted Arc*.

As noted earlier, Ahearn, like many other community-based artists, wished to create a work integrated with the site—a work that would seem to emerge so naturally from a particular place, whose meaning is so specifically linked to it, that it could not be imagined belonging anywhere else. But unlike the physical integration of the art-as-public-spaces paradigm (which Serra likewise rejected), Ahearn's community-based site specificity emphasized a social integration. This is in part due to the fact that the site itself is here conceived as a social entity, a "community," and not simply in terms of environmental or architectural design. But more importantly, the emphasis on the social stems from the belief that the meaning or value of the art work does not reside in the object itself but is accrued over time through the interaction between the artist and the community. This interaction is considered to be integral to the art work and equal in significance (it may even be thought of as constituting the art work). What this means is that the *artist's assimilation* into a given community now coincides with the *art work's integration* with the site. The prior goal of integration and harmony in terms of unified urban design is reorganized around the *performative* capacity of the artist to become one with the community. And this "becoming one," no matter how temporary, is presumed to be a prerequisite for an artist to be able to speak with, for, and as a legitimate representative or member of the community. Simultaneously, the characteristics of this "unity" function as criteria for judging the artistic authenticity and ethical fitness of the art work.

In most cases, community-based site specificity also seeks to bring about another kind of integration between the community and the work of art. A group of people previously held at a distance from the artistic process, under abstract designations of viewer/spectator, audience, or public, are enlisted in this case to participate in the creation of an art work. Sometimes this absorption of the community into the artistic process and vice versa is rendered iconographically readable, as, for example, in the literalist realism of John Ahearn's cast sculptures. At other times, when the art work is conceptually oriented, with priority given to the collective process and social interaction, with or without the guarantee of any material outcome, this absorption is more difficult to track. But a central objective of community-based site specificity is the creation of a work in which members of a community—as simultaneously viewer/spectator, audience, public, and referential subject—will see and recognize themselves in the work, not so much in the sense of being critically implicated but of being affirmatively pictured or validated.

This investment corresponds to an old imperative of public art: rather than art works that are separated or detached from the space of the audience, which reinforce social alienation and disaffection, one should sponsor works that reassure the viewing subject with something familiar and known. We can recall Janet Kardon's comment that in order for a public art work to be meaningful to the public (thus, meaningfully public), it should not "unsettle perceptions" but "reassure the viewer with an easily shared idea or subject."[86] In 1980, when these words were written, Kardon encouraged "sharing" through art that either performs a "useful task," such as providing shade or seating, or conjures an association with a "sense of leisure"—generic qualities she presumed to be desired and esteemed by all. In contrast, proponents of 1990s community-based public art have argued for the specificity of certain audience groups (i.e., communities), the basic sentiment being that the desires and needs of a particular community cannot be presumed to be so generic, and cannot be declared a priori by an artist or anyone else outside of that community. Therefore, the task of "reassur[ing] the viewer with an easily shared idea or subject" is best accomplished when the idea or subject of the art work is determined by the community, or better yet if it *is* the community itself in some way.

This principle holds true even in public art projects based in conceptual or performance art, which do not yield concrete material manifestations (that is, literal representations of the people of the community). For if we identify "the work" as the dialogue and collaboration between an artist and a community group, we conjure a picture of the community nonetheless, albeit in different terms, precisely of work. In eschewing object (read commodity) production, many community-based artists, often with the help of curators, administrators, and sponsors, orchestrate situations in which community participants invest time and energy in a collective project or process. This investment of labor would seem to secure the participants' sense of identification with "the work," or at least a sense of ownership of it, so that the community sees itself in "the work" not through an iconic or mimetic identification but through the recognition of its own *labor* in the creation of, or becoming of, "the work." Although the concept of labor rarely appears in public art discourse, and although the issue cannot be pursued in adequate depth here, it seems crucial to note the need to consider the representative function of labor within the context of community-based art practice generally.[87] For now, I can simply propose that the drive toward identificatory unity that propels today's form of community-based site specificity is a desire to model or enact unalienated collective labor, predicated on an idealistic assumption that artistic labor is itself a special form of unalienated labor, or at least provisionally outside of capitalism's forces.

But if the pursuit of identificatory unity, as I have described it thus far, is in part an updated means to "reassure the viewer with an easily shared idea or subject," the question remains: What exactly is reassured by it? And what does this reassurance guarantee? While it is not prudent to overgeneralize, a preliminary answer, pointing to both the hazards and hopes of contemporary public art, can begin with the observation that the viewer is affirmed in his/her self-knowledge and world view through the art work's mechanisms of (self-) identification. Underlying decades of public art discourse is a presumption that the art work—as object, event, or process—can fortify the viewing (now producing) subject by protecting it from the conditions of social alienation, economic fragmentation, and political disenfranchisement that threaten, diminish, exclude, marginalize, contradict, and otherwise "unsettle" its sense of identity. Alongside this belief is an unspoken imperative that the art work should affirm rather than disturb the viewer's sense of self. A culturally fortified subject, rendered whole and unalienated through an encounter or involvement with an art work, is imagined to be a *politically* empowered social subject with opportunity (afforded by the art project) and capacity (understood as innate) for artistic self-representation (= political self-determination). It is, I would argue, the production of such "empowered" subjects, a reversal of the aesthetically politicized subjects of the traditional avant-garde, that is the underlying goal of much community-based, site-specific public art today.[88]

While the complexities and paradoxes of current public art discourse remain unresolved, the need to rethink the operations of the existing models of site specificity is unambiguous. And the seeming failure of the two most recent paradigms—as exemplified in Serra's disruptive model based in sculpture, and

Ahearn's assimilative model based in community interaction—isolates some of the terms of that rethinking. *Tilted Arc* is a seminal instance of a nonassimilative, oppositional mode of site specificity that, while vilified by many, has been lauded by others for its critical capacity to challenge the prevailing tendency of public art to cover over the many contradictions that underlie public space. John Ahearn's project in the South Bronx, while contrarily an assimilative and integrationist effort, simi-

◂ Richard Serra, ***Tilted Arc***, Federal Plaza, New York, 1981–1989. (Photo by Susan Swidler; © Richard Serra/Artists Rights Society (ARS), New York.)

▸ Walton Avenue block party for inauguration of ***Back to School*** mural, Bronx, New York, September 3, 1985. (Photo by Ivan Dalla Tana; courtesy Alexander and Bonin Gallery, New York.)

larly illuminates the conflicted nature of the public sphere. If we are to measure a public art work's critical capacity in relation to the ways in which the work itself becomes a site of contestation over what constitutes something as public,[89] then the conflicts surrounding these two works underscore the lack of agreement over what we mean by, and expect from, an "interventionary" site specificity.

FROM SITE TO COMMUNITY IN NEW GENRE PUBLIC ART: THE CASE OF "CULTURE IN ACTION"

In the early morning hours of May 20, 1993, one hundred large limestone boulders, each about three feet tall and four feet wide and weighing roughly 1,000 to 1,500 pounds, mysteriously appeared on sidewalks, plazas, street corners, and parkways throughout the Loop in downtown Chicago. This odd and "spontaneous" outcropping of lumpy boulders on the streets of Chicago, each adorned with a commemorative plaque honoring a woman from the city (a total of ninety living, ten historical), was masterminded by Suzanne Lacy, a California-based artist best known for her feminist performances and protests from the 1970s. The event marked the unofficial inauguration of the temporary exhibition program "Culture in Action: New Public Art in Chicago." Sponsored by the nonprofit public art organization Sculpture Chicago[1] and conceived and directed by the independent curator Mary Jane Jacob, "Culture in Action" included seven other projects dispersed throughout the city at various neighborhood locations, all of which remained "on view" throughout the summer of 1993, from early May to end of September.[2]

Claiming to break from previous models of public art, "Culture in Action" took the entire city of Chicago as its stage and "focused on the active participation of residents in diverse communities in the creation of the artworks." According to its press release, "'Culture in Action' established a new vocabulary within the genre of urban-oriented sculpture exhibitions. . . . [It] tested the territory of public interaction and participation; the role of the artist as an active social force; artist-driven educational programming as an essential part of the artwork; and projects that existed over an extended period of time, not just as spectator-oriented objects for brief viewing."[3]

To do so, the eight projects included in "Culture in Action" were structured as community collaborations in which, with the help of Sculpture Chicago's administrative staff, the artist joined with a local organization or group to conceptualize

Suzanne Lacy and A Coalition of Chicago Women, ***Full Circle***, 1993. (Photos by John McWilliams; courtesy Sculpture Chicago.)

and produce the art work. The results of these collaborations were wide-ranging and hardly the typical fare of public art. In addition to Lacy's commemorative boulders (which was only one of two parts of her contribution to the program; part two consisted of a ceremonial all-women dinner), there was a multiethnic neighborhood parade, by Daniel J. Martinez, VinZula Kara, and the West Side Three-Point Marchers (Los Desfiladores Tres Puntos del West Side); a new candy bar designed and produced in collaboration with members of a candy-making union, by Simon Grennan, Christopher Sperandio, and the Bakery, Confectionery and Tobacco Workers' International Union of America Local No. 552; an urban ecological field station involving twelve high school students, by Mark Dion and the Chicago Urban Ecology Action Group; a storefront hydroponic garden to grow food for HIV/AIDS patients, by the collaborative team of Haha—Richard House, Wendy Jabob, Laurie Palmer, and John Ploof—with Flood, a network of health care volunteers; a street video installation and neighborhood block party organized with teenagers from Chicago's West Town area, by Iñigo Manglano-Ovalle, the Westtown Vecinos Video Channel, and Street-Level Video; the production and distribution of paint charts that reflect the lives of public housing residents, by Kate Ericson, Mel Ziegler, and a resident group of Ogden Courts Apartments; and a telephone survey project on name-calling, by Robert Peters with "Mushroom Pickers, Ghosts, Frogs, and other Others."[4]

Initially conceived by Jacob in 1991, "Culture in Action" (originally titled "New Urban Monuments")[5] was intended to be a critique of two institutions: the organization of Sculpture Chicago specifically, and more broadly the field of public art. Jacob's assessment of Sculpture Chicago's 1989 summer sculpture program showcasing ten relatively traditional sculptures on urban plazas[6] was not altogether favorable. Like most public art organizations, Sculpture Chicago's stated goals included demystifying the creative process and taking art to the "man on the street." But its effort to do so by presenting the artists at work in tents set up outdoors—so that the public could have "access" to their "creative process"—seemed to Jacob still to maintain a strict and rather naïve separation between the artist and the audience, between producer and spectator. According to Jacob, the board members of

Sculpture Chicago were shocked to be told, "You're fooling yourself if you think that by seeing a sculptor weld two pieces of steel together, somebody has a sense of what art-making is."[7] In fact, Jacob's desire to shift the role of the viewer from passive spectator to active art-maker became one of the central goals of "Culture in Action."[8]

Lauded by some as one of the most important public art events in North America in the twentieth century,[9] and criticized by others for its exploitation of communities and/or reduction of art to a kind of inadequate and ineffectual social work,[10] this project's scale and ambition, and the discussions it generated concerning the definition and function of contemporary public art, remain unrivaled in the post-*Tilted Arc* era. But the symptomatic aspects of "Culture in Action," particularly in relation to the problematics of site specificity, are most evident when we compare the Chicago program to another public art exhibition of similar scale and ambition, "In Public: Seattle 1991." Organized by Diane Shamash, then the Manager of the Public Arts Program of the Seattle Arts Commission (SAC), "In Public" showcased eighteen installations also sited throughout the city (sixteen temporary and two permanent).[11]

With funds made available in 1986 through the Percent for Art program during the construction of the new Seattle Art Museum, SAC solicited proposals from thirty local, national, and international artists that would "address, intervene in, and engage the public life of the city." This kind of approach, seeing the entire city and its processes as a site for artistic intervention, was not new to SAC. Indeed, it was SAC's formulation of the architect/artist design team concept for the Viewlands Hoffman electrical substation project in the mid 1970s that set an influential precedent for the urban design approach to public art throughout the 1980s.[12] "In Public," at the beginning of the 1990s, was an attempt to reassess the wisdom of imposing architect/artist collaborative structures, which by then had become extremely formulaic and restrictive, on artists wanting to work in the public realm.[13] So with the exception of the Pier 62/63 collaboration between architects Henry Smith-Miller and Laurie Hawkinson and artist Barbara Kruger, "In Public" granted individual artists the opportunity to initiate and direct their own projects, in locations of their choosing within the city, without necessarily having to collaborate with any design professionals.

"Culture in Action" made this feature a rule, eliminating the role of architects and design professionals altogether from the public art process. To a large extent, many of the stated goals of "Culture in Action" recapitulated the general terms of the Seattle program. "'In Public' was to be an experimental project that would push the boundaries of public art as we have come to know it and engage the public in a dialogue about the place and meaning of art in our daily lives."[14] But whereas "In Public" focused primarily on extending the types of public venue for artistic intervention, finding a broad range of unusual sites in and through the city (including newspapers, bus stops, piers, radio, television, as well as traditional public squares), "Culture in Action" abandoned the prevailing implication that architects and design professionals are expert negotiators between art and urban spaces. In effect, "Culture in Action" instead cast the "community" as the authority figure on such matters, privileging its role in the collaborative artistic partnerships forged by the program.[15]

Without question, what could be seen and documented as the outcome of "Culture in Action"—a candy bar, a neighborhood parade, a block party, a paint chart, a hydroponic garden, etc.—was in stark contrast to Chicago's own familiar forms of public art. Picasso's monumental cubist sculpture *Head of a Woman* (1965) on Richard J. Daley Center Plaza (also known popularly as the "Chicago Picasso"),[16] and the recent design of Pritzker Park by artist Ronald Jones (1991),[17] served as local prototypes against which "Culture in Action" established its newness and difference. Its difference was especially pronounced when one recognized that much of the work in "Culture in Action" was defined not in terms of material objects but by the ephemeral processes of interaction between the local participants and the artists. Furthermore, these interactions were not restricted, at least in principle, to the time frame of the exhibition itself.[18]

The 1993 presentation of "Culture in Action" thus exemplified on a grand scale what Suzanne Lacy defined as "new genre public art":[19]

> Dealing with some of the most profound issues of our time—toxic waste, race relations, homelessness, aging, gang warfare, and cultural identity—a group of visual artists has developed distinct models for an art whose public strategies of engagement are an important part of its aesthetic language. . . . We might describe this as "new genre public art," to distinguish it in both form and intention from what has been called "public art"—a term used for the past twenty-five years to describe sculpture and installations sited in public places. Unlike much of what has heretofore been called public art, new genre public art—visual art that uses both traditional and nontraditional media to communicate and interact with a broad and diversified audience about issues directly relevant to their lives—is based on engagement.[20]

"Culture in Action" affirmed Lacy's claim that "what exists in the space between the words public and art is an unknown relationship between artist and audience, a relationship that may *itself* be the artwork."[21]

The works in the exhibition also corresponded to what art critic Arlene Raven has identified as "art in the public interest."[22] According to Raven, art in the public interest is activist and communitarian in spirit; its modes of expression encompass a variety of traditional media, including painting and sculpture, as well as nontraditional media—"street art, guerrilla theater, video, page art, billboards, protest actions and demonstrations, oral histories, dances, environments, posters, murals."[23] Most importantly, she has argued, art in the public interest forges direct intersections with social issues. It encourages community coalition-building in pursuit of social justice and attempts to garner greater institutional empowerment for artists to act as social agents. Artists engaged in such art "aspire to reveal the plight and plead the case of the disenfranchised and disadvantaged, and to embody what they [the artists] view as humanitarian values."[24] Additionally, they "demand more artist involvement in institutional decision-making, representation of minorities and women artists, and use of the influence of museum and funding agencies to change government policies on social issues."[25]

Interestingly, the majority of those involved in such endeavors do not see their work within the historical framework of public art. Rather, they inscribe their practice—a contemporary form of socially conscious, activist political art—into the history of the aesthetic avant-garde. Raven, for example, cites Russian constructivism and the German Bauhaus as precedents for art in the public interest. She situates grassroots, artist-initiated activist groups from the 1960s (such as the Art Workers Coalition, Los Angeles Council of Women Artists, Foundation for the Community of Artists) as well as the alternative art movements from the 1970s within the same lineage, posing art in the public interest as a revitalization of the historical avant-garde's efforts to integrate art and everyday life.

Lacy likewise proclaims an alternative history for new genre public art. Disassociating it from the public art movement that developed through the 1970s and 1980s, she links it instead to the development of "various vanguard groups, such as feminist, ethnic, Marxist, and media artists and other activists . . . [who] have a common interest in leftist politics, social activism, redefined audiences, relevance for communities (particularly marginalized ones), and collaborative methodology."[26] According to Lacy, such interests lead to an attack on aesthetic categories bound to specificities of media, as well as the spaces of their presentation, and challenge the established criteria of cultural value based on aesthetic quality and individualistic notions of artistic competence. Thus, "draw[ing] on ideas from vanguard forms"—i.e., installation, performance, conceptual art, mixed-media art—new genre public art "adds a developed sensibility about audience, social strategy, and effectiveness that is unique to visual art as we know it today."[27] In so doing, it shifts the focus from artist to audience, from object to process, from production to reception, and emphasizes the importance of a direct, apparently unmediated engagement with particular audience groups (ideally through shared authorship in collaborations). According to Lacy, these artists, herself among them, eschew the constricting limitations not only of artistic conventions but of the traditional institutional spaces of their production and reproduction, such as studios, museums, and galleries. They choose instead the "freedom" of working in "real" places, with "real" people, addressing "everyday" issues. In a move one critic has dubbed "postmodern social realism," new genre public art also insists on a move away from the universalizing tendencies of modernist abstraction, to celebrate instead the particular realities of "ordinary" people and their "everyday" experiences.[28]

Foundational to this rhetoric of new genre public art is a political aspiration toward the greater "democratization" of art (a liberal humanist impulse that has always fueled public art). Qualities such as pluralist inclusivity, multicultural representation, and consensus-building are central to the conception of democracy espoused by the practitioners and supporters of new genre public art.[29] Rather than an object for individual contemplation, produced by a distant art specialist for an exclusive art-educated audience equipped to understand its complex visual language, new genre public artists seek to engage (nonart) issues in the hearts and minds of the "average man on the street" or "real people" outside the art world. In doing so, they seek to empower the audience by directly involving them in the making of the art work, either as subjects or, better, as producers themselves. By extending the hitherto specialized privilege of art-making and art appreciation to a larger number and broader range of people (not restricted to the privileged minority of the dominant class, gender, race, and sexual orientation), new genre public artists hope to make art more familiar and accessible (because it is now not only for the "public" but by the "public"). For the proponents of new genre public art, this ownership of art, or more generally cultural representation, is the basis for the integration of art and everyday life and a powerful force toward social and political change.

This effort to distinguish a "new genre" in public art might be approached critically as another form of aesthetic vanguardism, a renewed mode of social and political activism, or a new strategy of urban reform and revitalization. For some critics and artists, however, it represents neither a new movement in the field nor a newly politicized aesthetic sensibility, but rather a moment of arrival in which a well-developed mode of practice that had been undervalued in mainstream art finally receives broader cultural acceptance. According to Mary Jane Jacob, for example, this "new public art is not so much a movement of the nineties, a new way of working, as a way of working that has found its time."[30] Similarly for critic Eleanor Heartney, the major shift in public art as represented by "Culture in Action" is not so much a radical turn in practice as it is a belated turn in institutional reception. Citing Kate Ericson and Mel Ziegler, who claimed that "art has the ability to be a valuable social tool" and described their art as intending "to be pragmatic, to deal with pre-existing social systems and to carry on a dialogue with the public," Heartney has written with some enthusiasm: "Of course, such concepts have been part of certain artists' thinking and practice for years. Now, however, they have come out into the open, becoming stock-in-trade for art administrators, curators and critics as well."[31]

Whether understood as the development of something new or as the institutional acceptance of something old, the ascendance of this category of public art represents a significant shift within the public art field. For new genre public art not only insists on a reconsideration of (public) art's values and priorities along with alterations in its methodology and procedures; it also asserts a major rethinking of site specificity as a means to achieve its goals. In fact, advocates of new genre public art devalue, or at times explicitly reject, received definitions of the site and existing approaches to site specificity. The self-proclaimed radicality of "Culture in Action" in particular, and by extension the rhetoric and practice of new genre public art in general, depends on a fundamental redescription of site specificity's aesthetic necessity, its conceptual parameters, its social and political efficacy. Strangely echoing the arguments posed against the earlier site-indifferent models of art-in-public-places and art-as-public-spaces, many artists and critics now register their desire to better serve and engage the public, to further close the gap between art and life, by expressing a deep dissatisfaction with site specificity.

According to art critic Jeff Kelley, for example, "site specificity was really more like the imposition of a kind of disembodied museum zone onto what already had been very meaningful and present before that, which was the place."[32] Kelley is concerned here to conceptually distinguish "site" and "place," the former signifying an abstract location and the latter an intimate and particularized culture that is bound to a geographical region.[33] In associating the "site" with previous models of public art and "place" with new genre public art, Kelley means to highlight the limited social consciousness of site specificity as evidenced particularly in the art-as-public-spaces mode of practice.[34] At the same time, he registers the extent to which site specificity has experienced a radical reversal in recent years: where it was once a means to better integrate art into the spaces of the everyday, to better engage and accommodate the public, it has become a means to overrun the public and the meaningfulness of local places and cultures.

Such recent reassessments of site specificity, representing a fundamental rethinking of how an art work is to (or should) engage with its "public," turn on a crucial shift in which the "site" is displaced by notions of an "audience," a particular social "issue," and, most commonly, a "community." Artist Christopher Sperandio, for instance, speaking on behalf of the collaborative team of Grennan and Sperandio (one of the participants in "Culture in Action"), has unequivocally stated that they have abandoned the limited framework of the "site-specific" in favor of a more expansive notion of the "community-specific."[35] For Sperandio, the term "site" registers something neutral and implies a space that belongs to "someone else," i.e., an institution. A "community," in contrast, is apparently more specific and self-determined.

In a similar vein, Mary Jane Jacob has alternately described the projects in "Culture in Action" as both "issue-specific" and "audience-specific." According to Jacob, the move away from site specificity is a logical step toward a more intimate and meaningful relationship between the artist and his/her audience, a way of shrinking the distance between the traditionally separate poles of production and reception. "The commissioned works in 'Culture in Action' grow out of the alternative spaces and public art strategies of the 1960s. . . . They evolve as well from 'site-specific' artworks that, while tailored to particular locations, often remain discrete artworks within conventional exhibitions. In 'Culture in Action,' however, the artists' projects refer not primarily to sites, but to social issues that are of common concern to the artists and to the communities in which they have chosen to work."[36] Furthermore, "Each [project] is created in direct partnership with a local community and addresses such urban issues as low-income housing, HIV/AIDS research and care, workers' rights, minority youth leadership, ecology, and women's achievements. Such temporal, issue-specific artworks are a form of artmaking that grows out of the desire of artists to reach audiences in ways that are more direct and unexpected than is possible in a museum or gallery setting."[37]

Critics involved in the current public art debate have offered various conjectures on the nature of these changes. Dan Cameron, for example, has described the shift primarily as a stage in the development of a particular artistic genre. For Cameron, "Culture in Action" and other public art programs like it exemplify the general transformation of sculpture away from site specificity toward "post-site sculpture," toward an increasing dissipation of art as a cultural category.

> "Culture in Action" falls into the category of those sculpture exhibitions which have followed the logical progression from the model of site-specificity toward the apparent next stage: the dissolution of the language of "art" altogether, in favor of activities and interventions which take place directly in the community, away from the museum's watchful eye. . . . The work in "Culture in Action" set out to navigate that murky zone where social activism and post-site sculpture have begun to intersect.[38]

In contrast, Eleanor Heartney has characterized the current trend not so much as a logical progression in the development of sculpture but as a dramatic reversal in approaches to public art. Her argument positions the *Tilted Arc* controversy of the 1980s as a counterpoint to "the [recent] discussion [which] shift[s] away from the notion of site-specificity as a response to the formal dynamics of the site toward a concern with community as context." As she put it: "Before the construction of *Tilted Arc,* Serra announced that 'after the piece is built, the space will be understood primarily as a function of the sculpture.' Today, more often than not, the reverse seems to be true. Sculpture is seen as a function of the space or the context. Public artists tend to speak in terms of community participation, temporariness and the limitation of the authorial role of the artist."[39]

This last comment is more in keeping with Jacob's own conception of "Culture in Action." According to Jacob, the trajectory of the modern public art movement, within which her program marks a major turning point, plays out as follows:

> As public art shifted from large-scale objects, to physically or conceptually site-specific projects, to audience-specific concerns (work made in response to those who occupy a given site), it moved from an aesthetic function, to a design function, to a social function. Rather than serving to promote the economic development of American cities, as did public art beginning in the late 1960s, it is now being viewed as a means of stabilizing community development throughout urban centers. In the 1990s the role of public art has shifted from that of renewing the physical environment to that of improving society, from promoting aesthetic quality to contributing to the quality of life, from enriching lives to saving lives.[40]

Which is to say that, having lost its longstanding faith in the power of architecture and urban design to positively affect the quality of life in social terms, public art has reaffirmed its desire to impact the lives of (nonart) constituencies by other means. Instead of addressing the physical conditions of the site, the focus now is on engaging the concerns of "those who occupy a given site." These concerns, defined in relation to social issues—homelessness, urban violence, sexism, homophobia, racism, AIDS—ostensibly offer a more genuine point of contact, a zone of mutual interest, between artist/art and community/audience. The new formulation of community-based public art proposes a new partnership in place of the partnership between artist and architect valorized in the design team collaborations of the 1980s. The dialogue is now to occur between an artist and a community or audience group that is identified as such in relation to some social problem (which itself is often associated with marginalized and disenfranchised communities).[41]

The slide from site-specific to issue-specific in public art can be seen as yet another example of the ways in which the concept of the site has moved away from one of concrete physical location, as I argued in chapter 1. The invocation of the community-specific and the audience-specific, in which the site is displaced by a group of people assumed to share some sense of common/communal identity based on (experiences of) ethnicity, gender, geographical proximity, political affiliation, religious beliefs, social and economic classes, etc., can be described as an extension of the discursive virtualization of the site, at least to the extent that identity itself is constructed within a complex discursive field.

But the particular displacement of the site-specific by the community-specific in new genre public art requires special attention along a different trajectory of inquiry, because the prominence of community-based, participatory modes of art practice in recent years coincides with the frequent invocation of the community in many arenas outside the art context. Indeed, the community, generally understood as a collective body that mediates between individual subjects and society, has become a highly charged and extremely elastic political term. It is deployed equally by the left and the right to muster public support for certain social programs, political candidates, and legislative agendas; it carries weight in debates ranging from education and health care to housing policies and zoning regulations. On the one hand, the term "community" is associated with disenfranchised social groups that have been systematically excluded from the political and cultural processes that affect, if not determine, their lives. It defines coalitions of people seeking to counter such processes of exclusion and repression by collectively demanding equal rights, greater social recognition, economic support, and political power, such as the gay and lesbian community, the Asian American community, working-class communities, the African American community, women's groups, senior citizens organizations, etc. On the other hand, quite antithetically, the term is frequently invoked to describe departicularized identities of dominant social, economic, political, and cultural forces, such as the business community, the entertainment community, the medical community, the scientific community, the national and international communities. Furthermore, among neoconservatives the "community" is repeatedly conjured in efforts to instigate *new* exclusionary policies in housing, health care, social services, and education. In its drive toward the greater privatization of public institutions and services and the decentralization of state authority, the right has appropriated the concept of the community as well. The dismantling of certain state-sponsored social and cultural programs that especially benefit the poor and the ill, for instance, are carried out now in the name of community activism and community self-determination.

One example will suffice to illustrate the ways in which community-based rhetoric has become a flexible political tool for neoconservatives. In an article entitled "The New Community Activism: Social Justice Comes Full Circle," Heather Mac Donald describes the political struggles in the Lower East Side and the Upper West Side of New York City over the city's plans to locate in those neighborhoods new social service facilities for drug rehabilitation, mental illness, and AIDS treatment.[42] Detailing the opposition of a group of residents in each neighborhood to the city's plans, Mac Donald's narrative is marked throughout by her overriding concern to celebrate, as the title of her article indicates, a "new community activism." She begins her article with the ominous claim that "tolerance for the breakdown of public order under the banner of compassion and civil liberties is threatening the very survival of some New York communities." Against this perceived threat, she identifies "a new wave of community rebels who represent a revolution in the making. Citizens are rising to demand that the government stop dumping social problems onto their streets and start demonstrating a commonsense concern with the quality of life in the city's neighborhoods."[43] Thus, new community activism is characterized as a reclamation project—citizens taking back "their" streets and neighborhoods from both an inefficient government (the "therapeutic state") and those who constitute the social problems, who "gain money from the continued cycle of [state] dependence."[44] Rather than address the absolute necessity of social services for certain groups, Mac Donald writes only about the unfairness of social services being concentrated in particular neighborhoods.

For Mac Donald, the objectives of new community activism are twofold. First is the insistence that local communities, not government bureaucracies, have the right to determine the use of neighborhood spaces, for social services or otherwise, and that the community should be able to "control deviant behavior" within its purview without government interference. In other words, the community should have exclusive jurisdiction over the management of the spaces and resources of the neighborhood and be free to police the neighborhood against "unwanted" elements, such as drug addicts, AIDS patients, the homeless, and the mentally ill. But the larger battle is ideological. For Mac Donald's community activism is not only against government interference in community issues; it is about "bucking a long political tradition . . . that champions radical individualism, disparages middle-class values, and reserves particular contempt for 'gentrification.'"[45]

In a hyperbolic rendering, the liberal left is characterized as dangerously radical and oppressively dogmatic, either too sentimental and idealistic, thus irrational, or too corrupt and unreliable to offer any satisfactory solutions to deal with many of today's social problems. This is why new community activists must reclaim the term "community" from its supposed misrepresentations and misappropriations by the liberal left leadership. According to Mac Donald, "When social-service advocates talk of 'community,' they are using a code word that has absolutely no reference to real communities."[46] Not surprisingly, Mac Donald's notion of the "real" community is based solely on ownership of property; those who own (or sometimes rent) housing and real estate in the neighborhoods are the only legitimate members of the "real" community who can speak for its needs, management, future direction, and hopes. Consequently, the "real" community does not include or recognize the voices of others who might have contingent, nonproprietary relationships to the neighborhood, and it is delimited in finite rather than relational terms.

Much of the current effort of public art is in some measure a resistance to the strengthening forces of the right as exemplified in the case outlined above. In fact, participants in "Culture in Action" and proponents of new genre public art explicitly position themselves in opposition to such exclusionary tendencies. The highlighting of marginalized and disenfranchised social groups in community-based collaborative art projects is indeed an attempt to counter (if not compensate for) these groups' lack of social visibility and political power. And the endeavor to give voice to underrepresented and disempowered groups, often by engaging them in the very process of creating their own cultural representations, is understood by most of its practitioners and supporters as not simply an artistic experiment but a strategy of political importance.

According to critic Hafthor Yngvason, for instance, who participated in the December 1992 symposium on "Culture in Action,"[47] the political implications of the shift from site specificity to a collaborative, participatory mode of community-based practice are profound.

> As public art has developed over the last two decades, its emphasis has been on techniques of integration—not just to incorporate art physically into buildings and parks but also to foster social assimilation. While "site-specificity"—privileged in public-art circles as *the* public form of art—has provided a means to introduce art into neighborhoods without the glaring irrelevance of what has been called "plop art," it has rarely gone beyond the idea of responding to established ideas or "facts" about communities to participating in a public sphere where such facts can be examined and contested.[48]

Yngvason associates contrasting sociopolitical models with the "integrationst" and "participatory" modes of public art practice. Citing feminist political theorist Seyla Benhabib, he claims that the former is predicated on a vision of society as "'communities integrated around a single conception of the human good'—i.e., a conception that can be responded to in an unproblematic fashion and revitalized through simple design, such as a public plaza." The latter is based instead on a notion of society as "'marked by a "plurality" of visions of what is good, and of the good of association itself.'"[49] For Yngvason and others, to pursue the kind of participatory art practice that "Culture in Action" advocates is not only to critique the "medieval" notions of public art (understood as a coherent representation of a community permanently installed in a public square or public gathering place) but to resist the integrationst ideology in a political sense.

To test Yngvason's hypothesis, that is, to examine more concretely the aesthetic shifts in new genre public art in relation to their political implications for the community, we will turn to the specific conditions of the eight projects in "Culture in Action" and of the exhibition program as a whole. A critical interrogation of their various mobilizations of the term "community" will serve to elaborate on the function of the concept within new genre public art as it appears to engage the larger political debate concerning the future of democracy.

It will become quite clear that, despite the efforts of many artists, critics, and historians to unify recent trends in public art as a coherent movement, there are numerous inconsistencies, contradictions, and variations within the field, even within the "Culture in Action" program itself. In fact, the narrative of new genre public art's newness, as developed in significant part in the promotional rhetoric and critical reception of "Culture in Action," has continuously obscured or glossed over some of its most consequential inconsistencies and contradictions. For instance, while the wide range of artistic media and formal approaches in "Culture in Action" has been acknowledged, even celebrated, as a distinctive attribute of new genre public art's aesthetic "freedom," as evidence of its "experimental" nature, the fundamental differences in the social and political implications of the separate projects have largely been ignored.

Contrary to its curator's overarching program description, the projects in "Culture in Action" each present a divergent approach to the central problem of community engagement. But the differences among the projects in terms of their visual presentation reveal little of their conceptual and theoretical differences. These are embedded instead in the specific (invisible) *processes* of their respective community collaborations, in their *enactment* of the necessary institutional and individual exchanges and compromises (as opposed to their rhetorical descriptions of them), many of which have been carried out in improvisational ways. We turn now to these processes and exchanges—the complex set of relations and negotiations within the particular parameters of "Culture in Action"—in order to pose the following questions.

In actual practice, how does a group of people become identified as a community in an exhibition program, as a potential partner in a collaborative art project? Who identifies them as such? And who decides what social issue(s) will be addressed or represented by/through them: the artist? the community group? the curator? the sponsoring institution? the funding organization? Does the partner community preexist the art project, or is it produced by it? What is the nature of the collaborative relationship? If the identity of the community is produced through the making of the art work, does the artist's identity also depend on the same process? How does the collaboration unfold, and what precisely is the role of the artist within it? Does the partner community coincide with the audience? If new public art engages the audience as active participants in the production of an art work, which to a degree renders them subjects of the work, too, then who is the audience for *this* production? What criteria of success and failure are posed now, especially to the artists, in this major reconfiguration of public art that moves aesthetic practice closer to social services?[50] And finally, through it all, what are the political implications and consequences of new genre public art's simultaneous displacements of the architect and the site (once understood as a geographic location) by the community, the audience, and the social issue, as themselves different kinds of spaces?

* * *

The eight projects in "Culture in Action" can be grouped into four distinct categories based on the kind of interactions between the artist(s) and the respective community partner(s). The projects reveal varying degrees of intervention from the curator and/or Sculpture Chicago: some projects are fully dependent on institutional involvement; others are more able to oversee their own development. Each category also defines a different role for the artist, offering alternative renditions of the collaborative relationship. All in all, the variations among these collaborative models reveal the extent to which the "community" remains a highly ambiguous and problematic concept in public art today.

The first model is best exemplified in Suzanne Lacy's project *Full Circle,* with its hundred commemorative boulders. Here it is difficult to discern any community more particular than the social category of Women, despite the artist's effort to honor specific individuals from the city of Chicago. In preparation for the project, several committees of women were established by the artist and Sculpture Chicago to oversee the nominating and selecting of one hundred local women who would eventually receive a boulder commemoration. But the committees did not function as active creative partners in the overall conception of Lacy's project (at best, they were sounding boards for the artist's ideas). Instead, they were convened to perform and signify the decentralization of the artist's authority in defining the "content" of *Full Circle*—i.e., the names of individual honorees.

On the one hand, such a move seems logical, even commonsensical, as local residents would likely be more knowledgeable than the artist (from California) in assessing the social and cultural contributions of one of their own. On the other hand, Lacy's committee structure, employed as a means to humble the artist's voice and elevate those of local women, seems to confuse rationalized bureaucratization of the decision-making process with creative group participation. The artist's delegation of decision-making duties is not really the same thing as sharing of authority. Only those with authority in the first place are in positions to delegate; that is, the act of delegating is in itself an act of authority.

The committees, however, did infuse a sense of regional relevance to the project insofar as their focus was on Chicago residents. Lacy herself emphasized this aspect when she noted that "the invented nature of the nomination process grounded the project in the community and with the women selected."[51] This implies a locational delineation of the community. But what conceptually gathered all one hundred women into a coherent "community," or at least an extension of it, was not their common place of residence and work—the city of Chicago—or their presumed allegiance to it. Rather, according to Lacy, they shared a transhistorical, transcultural, and gender-specific "sensibility": "As the idea . . . grew, the issue that seemed to connect them was service—and a sensibility, whether through culture or nature, that seemed particular to women. 'Service,' an inadequate word, often challenged throughout the project, still seems the best way to describe a quality of supporting, nurturing, correcting injustice, promoting equality."[52]

Following this logic, Lacy orchestrated a conceptually coherent unity for all women, presumably identified with one another in the service activities of "supporting, nurturing, correcting injustice, and promoting equality." Granted, the model of unity here was not that of a cultural melting pot, with particularities of minority constituencies effaced or assimilated into the likeness of dominant social forces. In fact, Lacy emphasized the distinctness of individual identities—one woman, one boulder—over the importance of a single collective image. She made a concerted effort in *Full Circle* to model a unity of women that encompassed a wide diversity of professional backgrounds, ethnicities, social standings, ages, and religious affiliations, paying special attention to the inclusion of underrepresented and marginalized groups, such as African American, working-class, and older women. But whatever the individual differences, all were subsumed in the end by the artist's search for a common denominator that celebrated an abstract gender unity, delimited in this case by a set of service-oriented characteristics that were in effect naturalized as innate attributes of women in general. This was further emphasized by Lacy's symbolic all-women dinner, which augmented the project.

Within such a framework, the specificity of each woman's life drops out to a large extent (as does the specificity of Chicago), because diversity and difference are emphasized only to the degree that they can be overridden by a common principle or theme of unification. For example, the differences among the women in terms of their geographical attachments, socioeconomic position, cultural background, racial heritage, sexual orientation, and so on were absorbed by Lacy's notion of "service"—without taking into account the different relationships (social, economic, spiritual, emotional) that each woman might have to the very prospect of "service." Feminist social theorist Iris Marion Young has warned against reductive tendencies that would unite all women as nurturers and caretakers, especially when such characterizations are extrapolated into a gender-specific political vision.

> Despite our [feminists'] critical attention to much of the male tradition of political theory, many of us have retained uncritically an anarchist, participatory democratic communitarianism to express our vision of the ideal society. Indeed, many of us have assumed that women and feminists can best realize this ideal, because women's culture is less individualistic and less based in competition than men's culture, and because, we claim, women are psychologically and politically more oriented toward care and mutuality.[53]

As the artistic impresario of *Full Circle,* Lacy rendered an image of community that is an overgeneralized and abstract projection of commonality, a *mythic* unity that gathers into its folds a range of particular persons and their experiences. While her version of community diverges somewhat from the traditional ideal of a completely homogeneous and coherent social body, diversity and difference are articulated here only to be overcome or exceeded by a universalizing common goal.[54]

"Sited" Communities

The second model of community, perhaps the most prevalent in community-based public art today, is evident in the project by Simon Grennan and Christopher Sperandio and that by Kate Ericson and Mel Ziegler. In both cases, the artists paired with existing Chicago organizations, or "sited communities,"[55] that already had clearly defined identities in the sense of having established locational bases, modes of operation, or a shared sense of purpose. For Grennan and Sperandio the community partner consisted of members of the Bakery, Confectionery and Tobacco Workers' International Union of America Local No. 552. For Ericson and Ziegler the community partner consisted of representatives from the Resident Council of Ogden Courts Apartments. Being outsiders to the Chicago area, both artist teams required the assistance of, even became dependent upon, Mary Jane Jacob and the staff of Sculpture Chicago to provide local knowledge and access to such specific community groups.[56] In the end, Sculpture Chicago was not only instrumental in forging these partnerships; it served as the indispensable mediator between the artists and the local groups, especially during periods of the artists' absence from Chicago (which was most of the time of their yearlong affiliations with "Culture in Action").[57]

The point of departure for these types of collaborative pairings is most often signaled by the artist's project proposal. More precisely, the dominant thematic concern of the project as defined by the artist, and interpreted by the curator and the sponsoring institution, sets into motion the search for the "right" match, the "right" community group that can best fulfill the particular goals of the project. For instance, Grennan and Sperandio's collaborative liaison with the candy-making union resulted from a long search by the artists and curator for an appropriate partner who could fulfill the artists' desire to produce an "interactive artwork involving a community of Chicago-area manufacturing employees in the development and

Simon Grennan, Christopher Sperandio, and the Bakery, Confectionery and Tobacco Workers' International Union of America Local No. 552, billboard design for ***We Got It!***, 1993. (Photo by John McWilliams; courtesy Sculpture Chicago.)

marketing of a commercial product."[58] While Grennan and Sperandio conceded the need for further modifications to the project depending on the "specific nature and conditions of the hosting institution and workforce," the proposal specifically identified the outcome of the proposed collaboration—the production of a four-ounce chocolate bar, including its design and packaging.

In Ericson and Ziegler's case as well, the goals of the community collaboration, both in terms of material results and conceptual ambition, were established long before the engagement with any specific community group. In fact, in the preliminary outline for their project proposal dated June 14, 1992, months before a community partner was found, the artists described the overall configuration of the project in great detail.

> As we discussed our project still consists of creating a "color chart" in conjunction with a group of tenants from perhaps one or a few federally funded housing projects around Chicago. . . . Our plan would be to work with this group of tenants over the next year and develop this chart with the convention of other paint charts in mind. It would be a usable paint chart, distributed in paint stores throughout the U.S. . . . The chart would deal with some specifics about federally funded housing, demographics, etc. It would of course hopefully raise issues that are of concern to the tenants but it would also question the validity and morals of the suburbs which these charts often cater to. . . . Anyway, the charts soul [sic] purpose will not be to sell paint and these details will work themselves out during our collaboration.[59]

Within this model of community interaction, the artists in effect specify their community partners—in the case of Ericson and Ziegler, "a group of tenants from . . . one or a few federally funded housing projects around Chicago." The curator and the sponsoring organization (here, Sculpture Chicago) function as middlemen in facilitating the partnership. The artists can either find themselves assigned to a certain community group by the sponsoring agency or be given a list of groups to choose from. Thus, contrary to the promotional rhetoric that describes community collaborations as the result of an organic and dialogical relationship between the artist and the community, representing a set of mutual interests at the origin of the collaboration, the overall structure, procedure, and goals of the projects, including their conceptualization, most often precede the engagement with any such community. Jacob has claimed, for example, that "unlike other exhibitions of site-specific installation artworks that have merited recent attention, this project ['Culture in Action'] is the result of a fundamental collaboration among participating artists, community residents and civic leaders. This collaborative process has to an unusual degree shaped the conception as well as the realization of these artists' projects, and has led to a new dialogue between the artist and audience for public art."[60] But it is clear, at least in the cases of Grennan and Sperandio and Ericson and Ziegler, that the conceptual framework of the projects was fully articulated prior to any conversations with potential collaborators; the community partners instead came to fill the predelineated blank spots within that framework. The contribution of the community partners, in other words, was limited to the realization of projects that fully prescribed the nature of their participation in advance.[61] Elaborating on this particular point, many critics of "Culture in Action," in fact, have charged some of the artists, Jacob, and Sculpture Chicago with exploitation, even abuse, of local community groups.[62]

It is important to note in this context that Grennan and Sperandio informally proposed several different projects as viable options to Jacob, each proposal involving a different type of community group. According to Sperandio, it was Jacob who made the final selection among the list of six possibilities, in effect determining the project for them as well as proactively defining the community partner and the type of social issue that would be addressed by the project (in this case, blue-collar labor politics). This is again in contrast to Jacob's claim that the community collaborations in "Culture in Action" emerged organically through the initiatives of the individual artists working without specific guidelines or intervention. She has stated many times that the defining characteristic of "Culture in Action," including its testing of interactive community collaborations as a new model of public art, came into being in response to artists' own interests in socially oriented art projects, and that she and Sculpture Chicago, acting as disinterested agents, merely accommodated the artists' wishes and followed their lead. However, correspondences and official paperwork concerning the early planning of "Culture in Action" reveal that this was not completely true. Jacob and Eva Olson (executive director of Sculpture Chicago) directed, even insisted on, certain types of collaborations as an important means to establish the exhibition's identity. They not only sought out artists who wanted to do community collaborations but played a central role in defining the nature of these collaborations.

Some view this kind of interaction between the artist and the curator/institution as a form of artistic collaboration in its own right (as Jacob continues to do).[63] And it certainly can be. But it can also be viewed as an example of the curator's increasing, though often unacknowledged, involvement in determining the parameters of an art project, a streamlining of the creative process that leaves the artist with what Mierle Laderman Ukeles has called the "curatorial assignment."[64] The fact that Sperandio was unwilling to divulge to the author the plans for other possible community collaborations "rejected" by Jacob, on the grounds that these proposals will likely be realized in other cities within the context of other exhibitions,[65] further reinforces the view that community "collaborations" are often artist-driven and curatorially directed. Despite the public foregrounding and rhetorical elevation of the community in the discourse, in such cases the specific community group seems to perform a relatively incidental role.

The exchange between Sculpture Chicago and Elaine Reichek, a New York-based artist who was approached for possible inclusion in "Culture in Action," helps clarify how the exhibition tried to define "community collaboration." Reichek's preliminary proposal, dated August 7, 1992, described a project in which she would produce a number of embroidered samplers and a set of bisque commemorative pots in an installation at the Chicago Historical Society. The content of the samplers and the pots was to highlight local Native American history, emphasizing the voices of Native American women, who would be contacted by the artist via a local facilitator (Carol Becker of the Chicago Historical Society). These women's discussions of their personal histories and their thoughts on traditional museological representations of their culture were to be the basis for the content of the pieces in Reichek's installation.

Subsequently, attempts were made by Sculpture Chicago to forge a partnership between Reichek and a local Native American women's group led by Faith Smith of the Native American Service College, but without success. Perhaps unsurprisingly, the Native American women questioned Reichek's proposal with some suspicion, requesting the artist, if she was truly interested in their lives, to spend more time with them on their turf to develop a more intimate relationship before proceeding to represent them in her project. Reichek's proposal, which assigned the decision-making and "creative" parts of the installation (the selection of content as well as the determination of the final form and the actual act of producing the pots and samplers) solely to herself, was deemed by Jacob and Sculpture Chicago to be at worst self-serving, and at best too inflexible to accommodate the needs of the potential community partners. Consequently, Reichek was disinvited to participate in "Culture in Action" in September 1992. In a letter written by Jacob to Reichek around that time, the curator explained that the proposal did not allow for enough interaction between the artist and the community organization. Or, more precisely, it did not allow for a particular *kind* of interaction that "Culture in Action" wanted to sponsor. Jacob wrote, "It is essential to the exhibition of 'Culture in Action' that artists develop a work out of a community dialogue and involve others in the 'creation' of these public works. At the moment, I feel like we are at a deadend. I admire your work but do not want to force a change when the idea may be better executed by you alone."[66]

This early exchange with Reichek reveals the general ambiguity surrounding the very idea of collaboration: does the "creation" of a work mean the actual physical labor of making an art object (or component parts to a larger installation/ event), or does it mean the conceptualization of a project? This crucial question remained unanswered even at the end of "Culture in Action." There seems to have been an implicit division of labor in which the artist serves as the management (conceptualizing and organizing) to the community partners' actual physical labor on the "production line." In any case, the incident with Reichek highlights Jacob's role in determining the type of collaborations that would be supported within the context of "Culture in Action," even if at times the rationale for her decisions seem vague and their results appear contradictory to her stated goals.

Invented Communities (Temporary)

The third model of community interaction, exemplified in Mark Dion's and Daniel J. Martinez's projects, is one in which a community group or organization is newly constituted and rendered operational through the coordination of the art work itself. Also quite prevalent in current community-based practices, such an approach imagines the art work in large part as the effort involved in forming such a community group around a set of collective activities and/or communal events as defined by the artist. In Dion's case, the interaction was more or less based on a conventional pedagogical or educational paradigm. His Chicago Urban Ecology Action Group, which convened on a weekly basis during the one-year period of the artist's commitment to "Culture in Action," was set up as an extracurricular educational program with two local high schools. Dion functioned as the teacher/team leader of this special environmental study group of twelve students, whose activities, including a field trip to Belize, became synonymous with Dion's own artistic production.

Similarly, Martinez coordinated a new community group around/as his project. Named the West Side Three-Point Marchers, the group was composed of a network of members from several existing community organizations from the West Side area of Chicago (including school groups, community and religious centers, theater groups, neighborhood arts centers) who gathered for the single purpose of planning, organizing, and performing in a one-time event that Martinez envisioned for them—a carnival-like parade through three West Side neighborhoods on June 19, 1993. (This was one of two projects Martinez completed for "Culture in Action.")

In contrast to Dion's, Martinez's role in relation to the West Side Marchers was more like that of an artistic director, delegating certain logistical (and some-

Mark Dion and the Chicago Urban Ecology Action Group, ***The Chicago Urban Ecology Action Group***, 1993. (Photos by John McWilliams; courtesy Sculpture Chicago.)

times creative) duties to others, akin to Suzanne Lacy's mode of operation. Martinez's overall conception of the parade as a public event on the theme of immigration history and identity politics, within which local African American and Latino residents would represent themselves (to themselves), was the driving force behind the activities of the West Side Marchers, and this activity defined their group identity. The actual labor of forging the cooperative liaisons between the members of the various local organizations, however, was accomplished not by Martinez directly but by two local women, Angela Coleman and Elvia Rodriguez, residents of two key neighborhoods (one predominantly African American and the other predominantly Latino), who also oversaw the preparations for the actual parade itself. Whereas Dion conducted his classes more or less autonomously in response to the stated and perceived needs of the students, Martinez did not live in Chicago and had limited direct contact with the people who would be involved in his project. This meant that he was not only dependent on the institutional support of Sculpture Chicago to make the necessary contacts but was fully indebted to the sustained mediation of local insiders like Coleman and Rodriguez. These women's interpersonal skills, their familiarity with the residents of the neighborhood, and their willingness to cooperate with Martinez were all indispensable to the successful presentation of the artist's work.

Even more than projects that engage "sited" communities, those involving invented community groups such as these depend a great deal on the administrative and institutional intervention of the curator and sponsoring agency. Of course, the latter's intervention and support can open up unpredicted avenues for an artist to develop his/her project. Dion acknowledged this in a preliminary public statement about his project, for example:

> Why plan a project so complex that it spans several states and even countries and includes negotiating [with] organizations like The Belize Audubon Society, Arts International, The Brookfield Zoo, Providence St. Mel and Lincoln Park High School, World Wildlife Fund, The Department of the Environment, The Mayan Indian community,

Haha and Flood: A Volunteer Network for Active Participation in Healthcare, ***Flood***, 1993. (Photos by John McWilliams; courtesy Sculpture Chicago.)

Chicago's West Side to form Street-Level Video. Composed of fifteen teenagers, Street-Level Video was set up in cooperation with a local public access television station and an after-school program as an ongoing video workshop in which participants would work with the artist in creating videos that represent their own lives and concerns. Their collaboration on the videos extended from conception, preproduction, and postproduction to exhibition and presentation. During the public viewing period of "Culture in Action," for instance, Manglano-Ovalle worked with the Street-Level Video kids to plan a block party that included an outdoor video installation. The project was conceived as a semieducational inner-city youth program, with an emphasis on developing the participants' video production skills. Manglano-Ovalle introduced theoretical questions into their creative process, focusing on the students' relationships to urban territorialism, identity politics, cultural representations of youth culture, and mainstream media.

In the cases of both Haha and Manglano-Ovalle, the auspices of "Culture in Action" only served as the means to newly organize a sustainable community organization. The framework of the exhibition program provided the impetus for the creation of neighborhood and volunteer alliances—Flood and Street-Level Video—and helped to establish their internal structures and identities, but had little impact on their operation both during the sponsorship of Sculpture Chicago and after its termination. In fact, during the exhibition run, Flood and Street-Level Video maintained far greater independence from Sculpture Chicago than did other projects. And in outliving "Culture in Action," they exceeded their given status as community-based public art projects: their meaning and value defied the specific art-oriented contextualization of the exhibition.

One of the key reasons for their sustainability was the artists' intimate and direct knowledge of their respective neighborhoods and those living in them. As long-time residents of Chicago and as members of local community groups themselves, Haha and Manglano-Ovalle approached their projects with a realistic (rather than a hypothetical) sense of possibilities. They relied on preexisting personal ties to many of those who became participants in their respective art projects. And since the artists' collaborative relationships to the community partners were based

> The Parks Department, The Belize Zoo and Tropical Education Center, The Field Museum, and the airlines? Why—at least partially because I've got the Sculpture Chicago logistics team from hell behind me and that knowledge has at least partially determined the realm of possibility for the project's scope.[67]

But this means that the logistical support can also foreclose possibilities for the project as well. Insofar as invented community groups are conceptually and financially dependent on the art project for their operation as well as their reason for being, they have severely limited life spans; their meaning and social relevance are circumscribed by its framework as well. Without the exhibition, their continuation becomes untenable in most cases. Indeed, the groups that organized around Dion's and Martinez's respective projects, while suggesting a model for potential development in the future (especially Dion's high school environmental study group), dissipated rather quickly at the close of "Culture in Action" in September 1993.

Invented Communities (Ongoing)

The fourth model of community interaction is an offshoot of the third, the difference being in the community's sustainability beyond the exhibition context and its institutional support. Two projects in "Culture in Action," both (coincidentally?) by Chicago-based artists, fit this category. Haha—the artist team of Richard House, Wendy Jacobs, Laurie Palmer, and John Ploof—formed a volunteer group called Flood, dedicated to the building and maintenance of a hydroponic garden for the production and distribution of foods for AIDS patients. In addition, Flood transformed the storefront space in which the garden flourished into a kind of community center for AIDS education, networking with other health care organizations around the city to program weekly discussion meetings, public lectures, and special events.

Iñigo Manglano-Ovalle networked with existing community organizations and high school programs in his own predominantly Latino neighborhood in

Daniel J. Martinez, VinZula Kara, and the West Side Three-Point Marchers (Los Desfiladores Tres Puntos del West Side), ***Consequences of a Gesture***, 1993. (Photos by John McWilliams; courtesy Sculpture Chicago.)

Iñigo Manglano-Ovalle and Street-Level Video, ***Tele Vecindario***, 1993. (Photos by John McWilliams; courtesy Sculpture Chicago.)

on friendships and neighborly familiarity, the groundwork for a sense of trust and a fluid, dialogical mode of communication was already in place. Haha and Manglano-Ovalle began, in other words, as insiders with what one critic has called a "home-team advantage."[68]

This advantage freed Haha and Manglano-Ovalle from the kind of institutional intervention or assistance that many of the other projects in "Culture in Action" required, including the need for intermediary, third-party insiders to communicate with the artists' respective community groups, especially in their absence. The advantage of continuous and consistent contact between the artist and the community group throughout the year allowed for greater trust among the participants, permitting improvisational and spontaneous reactions to changing circumstances around the project. Pragmatically speaking, these local artists were able to address daily problems and misunderstandings more quickly and collectively (not intermittently via long distance), better integrating the art project into the flow of the everyday life of the participants. Through such a relationship, the artists and the community groups enjoyed a greater sense of collective ownership of the project, predicated on their capacity to better control the processes of their collaboration, the unfolding development of the project, and their final public presentations.

However, sustaining these projects after the withdrawal of financial and institutional support from Sculpture Chicago was not an easy task. Haha and Flood had to relocate the garden with the expiration of their lease on the storefront space at the end of the summer of 1993, which had a profoundly destabilizing effect. They never fully recovered, although other volunteer activities besides the maintenance of the garden continued for many months. At the time of writing, there is talk of restarting the garden with the cooperation of a local church. Manglano-Ovalle and Street-Level Video had an easier transition thanks to the foresight of the artist. Typically, equipment such as cameras, television monitors, and editing machines are loaned to artists or art institutions by corporations for the duration of a public art program or event. Familiar with such arrangements, Manglano-Ovalle successfully negotiated *permanent* donations of equipment to found an operative, ongoing video production studio. With the necessary equipment in hand, the participants of Street-Level Video were able to continue their work after the conclusion of "Culture in Action." The project exists in 2002 as Street-Level Youth Media, incorporated since 1995 as a nonprofit arts organization in its own right, with some of the original participants from 1993 serving as codirectors.[69]

* * *

This is not to say that collaborations conducted by local artists are bound to be more successful or meaningful than those by artists from elsewhere, or that only local artists can create sustainable projects beyond the temporary framework of a public art program, or that sustainability in itself is intrinsically of greater merit. Certainly, the quality of the interpersonal exchanges between artists and their community partners cannot be measured in such terms. Neither can the value of non-collaborative efforts, which do not aspire to address social or political conditions directly. It is true that local artists have a head start in terms of their familiarity with their area of operation—its geographical configuration, its history, its available resources, its constituencies. But none of this guarantees the success of a community-based project, nor is a permanent project necessarily more effective or valuable than a temporary one. In many instances, it may be the outsider's perspective that provides the more cogent and incisive contribution or intervention into whatever community issues are at hand.

With the idea of an artist's "home-team advantage," site specificity reenters the discussion in a new way, as the sitedness of the artist becomes one of the central points of contention in community-based public art. For some critics, the success or failure of a community-based art project rests precisely on the artist's status as either a sited insider (= success) or an unsited outsider (= failure). But the process is far more complex than can be accounted for by such a formulaic reduction. To be sure, the artist's relationship to a group of people, a particular neighborhood, or a city plays a crucial role in the type of collaborations that are logistically and creatively possible. But in each case the particularity of this relationship—of the artist's connection to the area and its people through geographical ties or past personal experiences—strikes a different balance in the triangulation (of power) between the artist, the sponsoring institution, and the chosen community group.

When the artist is from out of town, the sponsoring institution serves as a matchmaker and mediator, becoming the primary source of information and guidance for the artist. Sponsoring institutions like Sculpture Chicago, and their representative in the figure of the curator or artistic director, make the initial effort to introduce the artist to the potential local partner organizations, articulating to the latter the probable benefits of an artistic collaboration.[70] Often such an effort translates into selling a particular artist to a particular community group (usually by emphasizing certain aspects of the artist's exhibition history and his/her area of artistic interest), and vice versa. Even after a good working relationship has been established between the artist and a partner group, the agency continues to function as the conduit between them, helping balance the wishes and needs of the artist and the capacities and desires of the community partner.

In the case of a local artist, the artist usually functions as the primary point of mediation between the sponsoring institution and the community partner.[71] Whereas outside artists are most often associated with the institution (both are seen as outsiders to the community), local artists are usually identified with the community. Sometimes an artist will readily take up the role of community spokesperson. In other cases, the artist will function as a translator between the cultural realms of the art world and the local community group, shuttling back and forth between the two: here the *artist* performs the task of introducing or selling the public art agency and its programming agenda to his/her community partner group, and vice versa. In doing so, the artist engages in an ongoing process of describing and enacting his/her allegiance and commitment, constructing and maintaining a dual identity (as artist here, as community member/representative there).

Such a situation can leave the artist with a sense of isolation and estrangement in that his/her identity cannot be fixed to either side (there is always a remainder). But this is not to romanticize the role of the artist as a lonely outcast or to presume that the community and the art world themselves have stable identities. In fact, the uncertainty of identity experienced by the artist is symptomatic of identities of all parties involved in the complex network of activities comprising community-based art, including the community, the curator, and the institution. And, of course, all subjects within this network are internally split or estranged as well, continuously negotiating a sense of identity and subjectivity through differential encounters with the other. But this does not foreclose the possibility of generative discussions between contemporary art and the needs and interests of nonart constituencies. In fact, this instability of identity and subjectivity can be the most productive source of such explorations. In the next chapter, we will review the most salient critiques posed to community-based public art in recent years to further explore the ambiguous discursive power of the "community."

5

THE (UN)SITINGS OF COMMUNITY

In the essay "The Artist as Ethnographer," Hal Foster critiques the ways in which contemporary art has absorbed certain methodological strategies from anthropology, and deconstructs the "collaborative" interaction between an artist and a local community group in ethnographic terms.[1] In his view, the artist is typically an outsider who has the institutionally sanctioned authority to engage the locals in the production of their (self-) representation. The key concern for Foster is not only the easy conversion of materials and experiences of local everyday life into an anthropological exhibit (as "cultural proxies," as he puts it), but the ways in which the authority of the artist goes unquestioned, often unacknowledged.[2] While noting the aesthetic and political importance of innovative artist-community collaborations that have the potential to "reoccupy lost cultural spaces and propose historical counter-memories," Foster warns that "*the quasi-anthropological role set up for the artist can promote a presuming as much as a questioning of ethnographic authority, an evasion as often as an extension of institutional critique.*"[3] For Foster, a vigilant reflexivity on the part of the artist is essential if such reversals are to be avoided, because, as he paraphrases French sociologist Pierre Bourdieu, "ethnographic mapping is predisposed to a Cartesian opposition that leads the observer to abstract the culture of study. Such mapping may thus confirm rather than contest the authority of mapper over site in a way that reduces the desired exchange of dialogical fieldwork."[4]

Some of the economic, social, and political consequences of such a reduction can be extrapolated from Foster's comments. Just as the desire to engage "real" (nonart) places can prepare the way for the conversion of abstract or derelict (non-)spaces into "authentic" and "unique" locales ripe for development and promotion,[5] so the engagement of "real" people in community-based art can install new forms of urban primitivism over socially neglected minority groups. The "other" of the dominant culture thus becomes objectified once again to satisfy the contemporary lust for authentic histories and identities. "Few principles of the ethnographic participant-observer are observed, let alone critiqued, and only limited engagement of the community is effected. Almost naturally the project strays from collaboration to self-fashioning, from a decentering of the artist as cultural authority to a remaking of the other in neo-primitivist guise."[6] In this way, Foster argues, community-based artists may inadvertently aid in the colonization of difference—for benevolent and well-intentioned gestures of democratization can have effects of colonialism, too—in which the targeting of marginalized community groups (serving as Third Worlds found in the First World) leads to their becoming both subject and coproducer of their own self-appropriation in the name of self-affirmation.

Critic Grant Kester also takes up the problematic of the "collaborative" interaction between the artist and local community groups, but along a different theoretical trajectory, in his essay "Aesthetic Evangelists: Conversion and Empowerment in Contemporary Community Art."[7] According to Kester, the position of the community artist is analogous to the status of the delegate as described by, again, Bourdieu in his work on political semiotics, where the delegate functions as the signifier for the referential community, constituency, or party.[8] Bourdieu's analysis challenges the apparent naturalness of the signifying relationship between the delegate, who chooses or is chosen to speak on the community's behalf, and the community itself. While the delegate derives his/her identity and legitimacy from the community, this community also comes into existence politically and symbolically through the expressive medium of the delegate. Hence, Bourdieu argues against the common assumption that the delegate is a passive reflection of a preexisting political formation.

Following this line of thought, Kester questions "the rhetoric of community artists who position themselves as the vehicle for an unmediated expressivity on the part of a given community."[9] One of the effects of such presumption, Kester argues, is a potentially abusive appropriation of the community for the consolidation and advancement of the artist's personal agenda, in the same way that the delegate "confirms and legitimates his or her political power through the act of literally representing or exhibiting the community itself, in the form of demonstrations and other political performances."[10] In a characterization far more severe than Foster's, Kester compares certain collaborative community artists to a self-serving delegate who "claims the authority to speak for the community in order to empower himself politically, professionally, and morally."[11]

But what looks to Foster like an artist's ethnographic self-fashioning, and to Kester like a morally problematic identification perpetrated by the community artist, is often the result of institutional intervention and pressure. That is, the kind of reductive and equalizing association drawn between an artist and a community group is not always the work of a self-aggrandizing, pseudo-altruistic artist but rather a fashioning of the artist by *institutional* forces. A case in point is artist Renée Green's 1992 exchange with Mary Jane Jacob and Sculpture Chicago. In March of that year, by invitation, Green made a preliminary visit to Chicago to discuss her possible participation in the "Culture in Action" exhibition. Before the visit, Jacob and Sculpture Chicago, without consulting with the artist, prepared a brief biography and a sketchy description of *possible* projects by her and used these as promotional material to engage community organizations that they felt might be suitable as collaborative partners for Green. Jacob and Sculpture Chicago's interpretation of the artist's background, experience, and interests overtly emphasized her African American identity and isolated inner-city race conflicts as her primary area of interest (thus, as the likely subject matter for her public art project).[12]

The itinerary for Green's two-day visit, set in advance by Jacob and Sculpture Chicago, further reinforced this identification of her with an as yet unnamed African American inner-city community. Green's visit to Chicago was meant to identify several community groups that might be interested in participating in a public art project, with Green in particular, and conversely a community group that would interest the artist in some kind of collaboration.[13] But the itinerary, which was based on the recommendations of a book called *Passports to Black Chicago,* placed the artist in what she felt were extremely prescriptive and overdetermined situations: tours of selected African American ghetto neighborhoods, meetings with representatives from local African American cultural organizations.[14] The artist realized fairly quickly that her interest in pursuing the architectural history of the city, especially the legacy of Frank Lloyd Wright and his Prairie School, as a possible topic for a public art project was not in concert with Jacob and Sculpture Chicago's exclusive focus on her as an African American artist and their desire for a project that would highlight issues of urban racial conflicts or history. This institutional projection led to a parting of ways between Green and Sculpture Chicago soon after the artist's visit to the city.[15]

In such an instance, Green's itinerary, biography, and project description (all authored by Sculpture Chicago) can be seen as the first step in the curatorial and institutional delimitation not only of the possible community partners for an artist but of the type of project that might be developed between them (especially in terms of the social issue that it would highlight). Based on this and similar experiences, Green has said, "In some instances the curator attempts to anticipate the work of the artist based on the history of the site, and the work and identity of the artist. Often when the artist visits the site the curator will suggest things having to do with communities: 'I think maybe you would like to do something on this neighborhood.' For example, Fort Greene in New York or Chicago's Southside, a black 'community,' or a site associated with slavery."[16] Which is to say that the matchmaking mediation of the sponsoring institution, inevitably motivated by the presumption of an artist's interests and the anticipation of a particular kind of collaborative project, often reduces, sometimes stereotypes, the identities of the artist *and* the community group.[17]

This is not to say that artists and community groups are innocent pawns in a conspiracy devised exclusively by curators and art institutions. The important fact is that, within the community-based art context, the interaction between an artist and a given community group is not based on a direct, unmediated relationship. Instead it is circumscribed within a more complex network of motivations, expectations, and projections among all involved. Thus Kester's and Foster's critiques of community artists need to be qualified by the recognition of the central role that institutions and exhibition programs play not only in delimiting the identities of those involved, but in determining the nature of the collaborative relationship between them.[18] Moreover, all these identities—artist, curator, institution, and community group—are in the process of continuous negotiation. At the very least, their respective roles and actions need to be understood in relation to one another.

Nonetheless, the political implications of Kester's argument in particular remain provocative, especially since his scenario is quite antithetical to the celebratory ones offered by supporters of such practices like Suzanne Lacy and Arlene Raven. For Kester, the cultural mobilization of the social "usefulness" of art (foundational to community-based art) and the rhetoric that accompanies it need to be understood within what he calls the "moral economy of capitalism" and the history of liberal urban reform. He insists, "This outpouring of compassion and concern over 'community'"—imagined by many critical cultural practitioners as a means to greater social justice and inclusive political and cultural processess—"must be understood in relation to the successful assimilation in the U.S. of conservative arguments about the underlying causes of poverty, social and cultural inequality, and disenfranchisement."[19]

Characterizing recent community-based art as a kind of "aesthetic evangelism," and likening the function of community artists to those of nineteenth-century reformers and social workers, Kester argues that the prevailing logic of community-based art reproduces a reformist ideology that, like Victorian-era evangelism, envisions personal inner transformation and growth as the key to the amelioration of social problems such as poverty, crime, homelessness, unemployment, and violence.[20] Flagging a statement by Hope Sandrow of the Artist and Homeless Collaborative—"the practice of creating art stimulates those living in shelters from a state of malaise to active participation in the artistic process"[21]—Kester points to the ways in which community artists who address social problems or engage economically, politically, and culturally marginalized groups in their work overemphasize the primacy of individual transformation as a measure of their project's (artistic) success.

While the power of intimate personal transformation cannot be underestimated, such a focus, in Kester's view, naturalizes social conditions of poverty, marginalization, and disenfranchisement as an extension of an individual's inherent character flaw (lack of initiative, diligence, inner resolve, moral rectitude, self-esteem, etc.). So that in facilitating the production of "empowering" and "spiritually uplifting" community (self-) portraits—variously poignant, heroic, strong, united—the community artist may legitimate the presumption that the cause of social problems rests with spiritually and culturally deprived individuals rather than with the systemic or structural conditions of capitalist labor markets, stratified social hierarchy, and uneven distribution of wealth and resources. In this way, community-based art can easily obscure the effects of the broader socioeconomic, political, and cultural forces, including art initiatives themselves, that render certain individuals and communities marginal, poor, and disempowered in the first place.

Despite the accuracy of some of Kester's assessments, his economically deterministic reading of community-based art has led to charges of oversimplification. Artist Martha Fleming has pointed out that what critical projects like Kester's are addressing is not so much the actual practice of community-based art but one discursive characterization of it, its commodification and promotion as "new public art" by a "professional-managerial class (PMC)—the critics and curators currently creating careers and fiefdoms for themselves by harnessing and bringing into the fold an artists' activity that has been threatening the institutions that employ them."[22] While conceding the importance of Kester's work in bringing class and historical analysis to bear on current community-based practices, Fleming accuses him of contributing to a discourse that homogenizes the complex activity of such practices, excluding not only artistic precedents but "the hesitancy and doubt experienced by many artists working in this field."[23] To Kester's various characterizations of community artists as vehicles for the implementation of a conservative economic agenda, as pawns in the machinations of dominant political ideology, as victims of their own "corrupt" desire for fame through servitude, Fleming counters:

> But not all of us will so easily be made into inexpensive marketing consultants for disenfranchised communities abandoned by the state, or take the rap for the failure of the welfare state. . . . In some cases our artistic practice has come out to meet our social activism.

> In other cases, a sense of specific, personal identification with civil and human rights issues has nurtured our practice. . . .We are from inside the belly of the beast trying to be responsible for and to people and things seriously wronged and wrong, that need work all around us in our immediate environment.[24]

This exchange between Kester and Fleming in the pages of *Afterimage* throws into relief some of the fault lines within the discourse of community-based art. On the one hand, Kester points to the problem of overidentification, even disingenuous misidentification, of the artist with his/her community. In his account, the institutional agenda and the role of the curator tend to drop out, as already noted, and the artist emerges as the primary protagonist, either complicitous with or at the mercy of dominant economic and political agendas. In the meantime, community groups themselves, usually understood as victims of society, are typecast as having little or no agency (Kester characterizes them at one point as "atomized social detritus of late capitalism").[25] Even as he criticizes community artists for such typecasting, he does the same in his own analysis insofar as community groups remain passive, almost silent entities upon which artists ostensibly perform their transformative magic.

On the other hand, Fleming, in identifying with community-based groups and causes and in placing herself and her work outside the conventional art context—"in the belly of the beast" as she puts it—distances herself from critics and curators, whom she makes equally culpable agents of an authoritarian and exclusive art world ideology. She blames the practices of mainstream art institutions (museums, academia, criticism, the market) and their representatives (curators, historians, critics, dealers, collectors) for sustaining the agendas of the dominant culture and ignoring the efforts of artists like herself who would question or challenge it. Ironically, her argument casts community artists as victims (perennially ignored and unrewarded by an exclusive and commercially oriented art world), validating to some degree Kester's conclusions regarding the processes of (mis)identification and transference between the artist and marginalized community groups. It is perhaps not surprising that Fleming excludes the artist from the category of the professional-managerial class (PMC) with whom she obviously *dis*identifies. This seems willful, though, since it has become more and more evident in recent years to what extent artists function in administrative and managerial capacities in relation to, or as a form of, site-oriented, project-based art.[26]

* * *

Such complex geometries of identification, misidentification, and disidentification, as well as the accompanying reductivism and counterreductivism (if not recrimination), often obscure the central issue at hand, which is the discursive construction of the community itself. While the ethical dimensions of community-based art, in particular the nature of the interaction between the artist and the community, and the aesthetic and social merit of community-based art are debated at length, the notion of community is very much overlooked. Even in complex analyses such as Fleming's and Kester's, the operative definition of the community remains minimally articulated. Generally speaking, an unquestioned presumption designates the community as a group of people identified with each other by a set of common concerns or backgrounds, who are collectively oppressed by the dominant culture, and with whom, in the context of community-based art, artists and art agencies seek to establish a collaborative relationship (to address if not challenge this oppression).

To be fair, Kester does make an important distinction between preexisting, "politically-coherent" communities and those that are "created" through the delegate-artist for the fulfillment of an art project. In his view, a collaboration in the latter case tends to be fraught with paternalism, because the participants who make up the community are defined as "socially isolated individuals whose ground of interconnection and identification as a group is provided by an aesthetically ameliorative experience administered by the artist."[27] In contrast, collaborations with "politically-coherent" communities yield a more "equitable process of exchange and mutual education, with the artist learning from the community and having his or her own presuppositions (about the community and the specific social, cultural, and political issues) challenged and expanded."[28] According to Kester, self-determined identities of "politically-coherent" communities are derived from an ongoing collective process of internal debate and consensus formation around issues of common interest to their members. Defined primarily by shared cultural traditions and a shared sense of struggle against different modes of oppression (racist, sexist, classist, etc.), these communities are more resistant to appropriation and abuse by the artist and the art world.

There are several problems with this formulation. First, its identification of communities in terms of *prior* "coherence" discounts the ways in which artists can help engender different types of community. As I tried to show in the previous chapter, an art project can be an important catalyst for the development of new alliances and coalitions, however temporary (e.g., Iñigo Manglano-Ovalle and Street-Level Video, Haha and Flood, and to some degree Mark Dion and the Chicago Urban Ecology Group). Moreover, quite contrary to Kester's conclusions, many collaborative projects reveal the extent to which "coherent" communities are *more* susceptible to appropriation by artists and art institutions precisely because of the singular definition of their collective identities (e.g., Grennan and Sperandio and the candy-making union; Ericson and Ziegler and the resident group at Ogden Courts Apartments). In fact, certain types of community groups are now very often favored for artistic partnerships because of the easy correspondence between their identity and particular social issues. The practical benefits of such an approach for some artists as well as most sponsoring institutions (less ambiguity, more control over the process of collaboration, more predictability and easier projection of outcome, facility in promotion and instrumentalization) have already led to the popularization of newly bureaucratized and formulaic versions of community-based art: artist + community + social issue = new critical/public art.[29] In such circumstances, the identity of a community group comes to serve as the thematic content of the art work, representing this or that social issue in an isolated and reified way. In the process, the community itself can become reified as well.

Secondly, Kester's argument implicitly supports the essentialism that undergirds the frequently voiced belief that only local artists—from the community, from the neighborhood, from the city: that is, artists with a "home-team advantage"—are fit to conduct genuinely meaningful community-based work. Even though he insists on the need to understand the unity of a community as "the product of contingent processes of identification,"[30] when he categorizes two different types of communities and two corresponding collaborative results, one good and one bad, he argues in effect against the "authenticity" (thus, legitimacy or effectiveness) of a community that might be activated as a result of a collaborative art process. In so doing, he disallows the important ways in which an artistic intervention can productively reinvent or critique the very concept of a community.[31]

Kester's critical effort reflects the difficulties of defining an operative definition of the community in today's art context. Typically, the objectives and identity of a coherent community are seen as determined by its members before any encounter with outside individuals or groups, including community artists. Additionally, the community is primarily defined in opposition to the forces of an oppressive dominant culture that would regulate and defuse the efforts of those who seek greater participation in the existing social system.[32] This focus on the oppositional character of a community supports the habitual tendency among artists and art professionals to think of the "community" as a synonym for social groups of the marginal or underprivileged classes. It has become commonplace in public art to cast the community as the victimized yet resilient other that continuously tests the stability of prevailing sociopolitical and economic conditions. Such a conception of community also reinforces the classic Marxist view that refuses to acknowledge the ways in which the "oppression" by the dominant class can actually ensure the coherence of a minority group.

But as I argued in the previous chapter, the notion of community is equally available to neoconservative "activism" that defends actions, even violations, against underprivileged and disenfranchised minority groups.[33] This suggests that the "community," coveted in contemporary political, economic, social, and cultural discourses alike, is not bound to any particular class, gender, ethnicity, age group, religion, location, or even type of cause. Insofar as its invocation can serve a broad range of purposes, for the liberal left and the conservative right, and designate a wide array of group types, its rhetorical uses today are fraught with more ambiguity and flexibility than are accounted for by either advocates or critics of community-based art. Perhaps in recognition of this general problem, Kester recommends that community artists (critics, too?) should "address each case of artist/community interaction as a specific constellation of difference (subject of course to broader, more socially and culturally consistent trajectories of difference and privilege), that requires its own strategic response."[34] Martha Fleming also notes that "there are many different kinds of community, activism, audience, and public, and many different meanings for each of these words, and all must be examined in their particular, unique contexts."[35]

Certainly, the issue of difference is key to any understanding of identity formation, collective and otherwise. It is also an important key to understanding the possibilities and limitations of community-based art. But the concept of difference suggested by these authors reduces it to the idea of multiplicity of uniquenesses, indicating simply the acknowledgment of the existence of diverse particularities within contemporary society. That is, whether characterized as mostly inaccessible to anything beyond an exploitative appropriation by an artist (as in Kester's scenario), or as available to genuine collaboration that naturally extends an artist's realm of operation to the mutual benefit of all those involved (as in Fleming's), diverse particular communities seem fully formed entities, awaiting engagement from the outside. Though not altogether without political and artistic efficacy, such a conception of difference supports a temporal and spatial demarcation of community formation that renders communities into discrete social formations.

Political theorist Chantal Mouffe has called this conception "a closed system of differences,"[36] wherein difference is understood not as a process of continual identification/(mis)recognition and alienation/(mis)recognition intrinsic to the (self-) construction of identity and subjectivity—that is, as a complex relational process—but as a series of distinct social categories that can sometimes be held together by a broader unifying ideal (such as the People, the Nation, or Women, as was the case in Suzanne Lacy's *Full Circle* project for "Culture in Action"). Difference understood accordingly as variety of social and cultural categories is an underlying presumption of community-based art today, which seeks to become ever more inclusive of this variety at the expense of a rigorous and self-critical examination of the primary driving force that seems to define the field—the *idealized specter* of community.[37]

* * *

The ideal of community, according to feminist social theorist Iris Marion Young, is a dream that "express[es] a desire for selves that are transparent to one another, relationships of mutual identification, social closeness and comfort."[38] The strength and seductiveness of such a dream rests on its promise of a "good society" that can counter the experiences of alienation and disassociation (and the accompanying social problems) that characterize life in contemporary urban mass societies. But for Young the ideal of community is a highly problematic proposition, because it typically envisions "small, face-to-face, decentralized units" as the preferred scale of interaction for all social relations, which is impossible in a practical sense in our postindustrial mass urban societies—fundamentally a nostalgic fantasy of a preurban existence that is assumed to have been without alienation, mediation, or violence. More importantly, the ideal of community is untenable to Young because it "privileges unity over difference, immediacy over mediation, sympathy over recognition of limits of one's understanding of others from their point of view."[39]

The ideal of community, in her view, is predicated on an ideal of shared or fused subjectivities in which each subject's unified coherence is presumed to be not only transparent to him/herself but identically transparent to others.[40] Such fantasies of transparent, unmediated, and transcendent knowing, Young notes, participate in the "metaphysics of presence" or "logic of identity" (theorized by Theodor Adorno and Jacques Derrida) that overlooks difference between subjects and denies difference as a constitutive element in the process of subject formation. Moreover, "the desire for social wholeness and identification" through mutual affirmation, closeness, and reciprocity as expressed in the ideal of community obscures the extent to which it "generates borders, dichotomies, and exclusions."[41] As such, the community ideal partakes of the "same desire for social wholeness and identification that underlies racism and ethnic chauvinism on the one hand and political sectarianism on the other."[42] In short, the ideal of community finds comfort in the neat closure of its own homogeneity.

Toward the conclusion of her argument, Young remarks that it may be politically expedient to drop the term "community" altogether in favor of "a politics of difference." Unfortunately, and surprisingly, she does not push the concept of a "politics of difference" any farther than "social relations that embody openness to unassimilated otherness with justice and appreciation."[43] Her proposal remains simply a call for greater tolerance of differently identified social groups—a proposal for an "unoppressive" society "without domination in which persons live together in relations among strangers with whom they are not in community."[44] As if abandoning the finer points of her own deconstructive analysis, she ends with a plea that basically amounts to "let's all get along." Difference, described initially as a socially mediated work in process, returns to a stable and fixed identity.[45]

Nonetheless, aspects of Young's critique of the ideal of community—its reliance on unified subjects, its assumption of a transparency of identity and subjectivity (i.e., self-presence), its fortification of a homogeneous group formation through the repression of difference, etc.—remain very useful in unpacking some of the hidden premises of community-based art. In fact, all the projects in our case study "Culture in Action" are infected to varying degrees by the kinds of presumptions that Young critiques. For instance, when Mary Jane Jacob and Sculpture Chicago presumed an automatic affinity between Renée Green and the African American inner-city cultural organizations of Chicago, the presumption was based on the belief that the artist's heritage, her African American racial identity, would facilitate, if not guarantee, a direct and authentic point of identification between the artist and the community. Whether the point of unity and mutual identification between artist and community group was imagined to be race and gender identity (Suzanne Lacy's rock commemorations to women, Daniel Martinez's parade through Latino and black neighborhoods, Iñigo Manglano-Ovalle's street-level video program with Latino gang members and "at-risk" youth), or shared interest in a particular social issue, such as workers' rights (Grennan and Sperandio's *We Got It!* candy bar), home and housing (Ericson and Ziegler's *Eminent Domain* paint chart), health care and AIDS activism (Haha and Flood's storefront garden), or ecological conservation (Mark Dion and the Chicago Urban Ecology Group), "Culture in Action" promoted a kind of reductive identification between the "collaborators" throughout its programming.

This is a typical essentializing process in community-based art: the isolation of a single point of commonality to define a community—whether a genetic trait, a set of social concerns, or a geographical territory—followed by the engineering of a "partnership" with an artist who is presumed to share this point of commonality. A logic of transparency based on the presumption of unified subjects guides such programming. The resulting collaborative art project based on this reduced point of identification or affiliation is then presented as conveying the identity of the community itself. Put another way, the identity that is *created* by the art project is viewed as a self-affirming, self-validating "expression" of a unified community (of which the artist ostensibly is now an integral part), as if the community or any collective group (or any individual subject) could be fully self-present and able to communicate its self-presence to others with immediacy. What remain invisible in the process are the mediating forces of the institutional and bureaucratic frameworks that direct such productions of identity, and the extent to which the identity of such institutional forces are themselves in continuous process of (re)articulation.

For some artists, the institutional and bureaucratic frameworks that rationalize and instrumentalize the collective experience in community-based art make it an unacceptable mode of practice for anyone interested in challenging the dominant social order. Beyond the difficulty of defining the term "community," the problem for artists like Critical Art Ensemble (CAE) lies in the impossibility of forging a collaborative affiliation based on truly nonrational aspects of human interaction, such as friendship, faith, trust, and love, within the existing models of community-based practice. CAE puts it this way:

> Assuming that an artist has successfully navigated the cultural

> bureaucracy and acquired money for a community project . . . just how will s/he insinuate h/erself into a "community"? The easiest way is to have the project mediated by a bureaucracy that claims to represent the community. A school, a community center, a church, a clinic, etc., is then selected, often because it is willing to participate in the project. The bureaucratic experts from the selected institution will represent the community and tailor the project to their specifications in a negotiation that also accounts for the desires of the artist. When the process is over, who has actually spoken? Since the majority of the negotiation over *policy* is not done with individuals in the territory, but with those who claim to represent it, which is again shaped by the bureaucratic parameters placed on the project by the money donors, how much direct autonomous action is left? How much dialogue has taken place? Not much. What is left is the representation of a representation (the bureaucratic opinion of the artist and h/is mediators).[46]

CAE's negative assessment of community-based art allows no qualifications: "Artworks which depend on bureaucracy in order to come to fruition (i.e., institutionally sanctioned public art including community-based art) are too well managed to have any contestational power. In the end they are acts of compliance that only reaffirm hierarchy and the rational order."[47]

CAE's position, while not without its own brand of avant-gardist romanticism regarding the place and mode of "resistant" critical art practice,[48] expresses a central complication plaguing community-based art: the conversion of attempts at a participatory model of art practice, engaging local concerns and people, into yet another form of acquiescence to the powers of capital and the state. Indeed CAE's characterization of this process is not altogether an exaggeration. But to abandon the entire enterprise in the belief that artists have no way out—because every attempt will end in falsehood and complicity—is perhaps prematurely defeatist.

Without doubt, artists, critics, curators, art institutions, and funding organizations are pressured today to think and act as if communities exist as coherent social entities awaiting outreach. The field continues to covet images of coherence, unity, and wholeness as the ideal representation of a community. (In a sense, the shift in focus from public spaces to local cultures has not displaced the ideology of unity that has prevailed in [public] art over the past three decades.) While such an outlook contributes to some expansion of art audiences, strengthening the tie between elite cultural institutions and local constituencies normally disengaged from their activities, its effects also include the reification and colonization of marginal, disenfranchised social groups, as well as the concomitant reification and commodification of local cultures. Furthermore, as some artists have noticed, community-based art can function as a kind of "soft" social engineering to defuse, rather than address, community tensions and to divert, rather than attend to, the legitimate dissatisfaction that many community groups feel in regard to the uneven distribution of existing cultural and economic resources. Additionally, according to artist Iñigo Manglano-Ovalle, there "is a growing and disturbing similarity between initiatives such as community policing and [community-based] cultural programs," both motivated at times by a paranoiac fear of social upheaval.[49] Which is to say, community-based art "on the streets," despite the "real-life" siting, serves a disciplinary purpose just as do art museums.

As the artistic, political, and ethical pitfalls of community-based art become more visible and more theorized, the need to imagine alternative possibilities of togetherness and collective action, indeed of collaboration and community, becomes more pronounced. Even to begin thinking about these alternatives, however, requires a major reconceptualization of the "community." French philosopher Jean-Luc Nancy has defined some guidelines for such an endeavor: "there is no communion, there is no common being, but there is being *in* common";[50] "the question should be the community of being and not the being of community."[51] In Nancy's overall project, according to George Van Den Abbeele, "community is neither a community of subjects, nor a promise of immanence, nor a communion of individuals in some higher or greater totality. . . . It is not, most specifically, the product of any work or project; it is *not* work, not a product of projected labor, nor an *oeuvre,* but what is un-worked, *dés-oeuvré.*"[52]

The challenge, then, is to figure out a way beyond and through the impossibility of community.[53] This is not to invoke a transcendent plateau from which one will find a new synthetic resolution free of contradictions. Quite the contrary, it is meant to suggest the impossibility of total consolidation, wholeness, and unity—in an individual, a collective social body like the "community," or an institution or discipline—and, perhaps more importantly, to suggest that such an impossibility is a welcome premise upon which a *collective artistic praxis,* as opposed to "community-based art," might be theorized.[54]

Community-based art, as we have seen, is typically understood as a *descriptive* practice in which the community functions as a referential social entity. It is an other to the artist and the art world, and its identity is understood to be immanent to itself, thus available to (self-) expression. The degree of success of an art project of this kind is measured in relation to the extent to which these (self-) expressions, as signifiers of community identity, affirm rather than question the notion of a coherent collective subject. The mirage of this coherence, fortified by the fact that the representation of the community is ostensibly produced with or by the same, is consumed as authenticity.

In contrast, collective artistic praxis, I would suggest, is a *projective* enterprise. It involves a provisional group, produced as a function of specific circumstances instigated by an artist and/or a cultural institution, aware of the effects of these circumstances on the very conditions of the interaction, performing its own coming together and coming apart as a necessarily incomplete modeling or working-out of a collective social process.[55] Here, a coherent representation of the group's identity is always out of grasp. And the very status of the "other" inevitably remains unsettled, since contingencies of the negotiations inherent in collaborative art projects—between individuals within the group, between the group and various "outside" forces—would entail the continuous circulation of such a position. Such a praxis also involves a questioning of the exclusions that fortify yet threaten the group's own identity.

This is not necessarily to assert incoherence, ambiguity, and uncertainty as deeper truths of identity. But it is in part what I understand Nancy to mean by the community as "un-working" or "inoperative"—the idea that only a community that questions its own legitimacy is legitimate. Reckoning with the impossibility of community, and consequently redefining community-based art as collective artistic praxis as sketched above, may be the only way to imagine past the burden of affirmational siting of community to its critical unsiting.

6

BY WAY OF A CONCLUSION: ONE PLACE AFTER ANOTHER

> *The bulldozing of an irregular topography into a flat site is clearly a technocratic gesture which aspires to a condition of absolute* placelessness, *whereas the terracing of the same site to receive the stepped form of a building is an engagement in the act of "cultivating" the site.*
>
> *This inscription . . . has a capacity to embody, in built form, the prehistory of the place, its archeological past and its subsequent cultivation and transformation across time. Through this layering into the site the idiosyncrasies of place find their expression without falling into sentimentality.*
>
> —Kenneth Frampton[1]

> *The elaboration of place-bound identities has become more rather than less important in a world of diminishing spatial barriers to exchange, movement and communication.*
>
> —David Harvey[2]

It occurred to me some time ago that for many of my art and academic friends, the success and viability of one's work are now measured by the accumulation of frequent flyer miles. The more we travel for work, the more we are called upon to provide institutions in other parts of the country and the world with our presence and services, the more we give in to the logic of nomadism, one could say, the more we are made to feel wanted, needed, validated, and relevant. Our very sense of self-worth seems predicated more and more on our suffering through the inconveniences and psychic destabilizations of ungrounded transience, of not being at home (or not having a home), of always traveling through elsewheres. Whether we enjoy it or not, we are culturally and economically rewarded for enduring the "wrong" place. We are out of place all too often. Or, perhaps more accurately, the distinction between home and elsewhere, between "right" and "wrong" places, seems less and less relevant in the constitution of the self.

As many cultural critics and urban theorists have warned, the intensifying conditions of such spatial undifferentiation and departicularization—fueled by an ongoing globalization of technology and telecommunications to accommodate an ever-expanding capitalist order—exacerbate the effects of alienation and fragmentation in contemporary life.[3] The drive toward a rationalized universal civilization, engendering the homogenization of places and the erasure of cultural differences, is in fact the force against which Frampton proposes a practice of "critical regionalism" as described in this chapter's first epigraph—a program for an "architecture of resistance." If the universalizing tendencies of modernism undermined the old divisions of power based on class relations fixed to geographical hierarchies of centers and margins only to aid in capitalism's colonization of "peripheral" spaces, then the articulation and cultivation of diverse local particularities is a (postmodern) reaction against these effects. Henri Lefebvre has remarked: "Inasmuch as abstract space [of modernism and capital] tends towards homogeneity, towards the elimination of existing differences or peculiarities, a new space cannot be born (produced) unless it accentuates differences."[4]

It is perhaps no surprise, then, that the efforts to retrieve lost differences, or to curtail their waning, become heavily invested in reconnecting to uniqueness of place—or more precisely, in establishing authenticity of meaning, memory, histories, and identities as a *differential function* of places. This differential function associated with places, which earlier forms of site-specific art tried to exploit and which the current incarnations of site-oriented works seek to reimagine, is the hidden attractor in the term "site specificity." The mobilization of site-specific art from decades ago, and the nomadism of artists in recent site-oriented practices, can be viewed alike as symptomatic of the dynamics of deterritorialization as theorized in urban spatial discourse.

In contemporary art discourse, one of the dominant positions on this phenomenon is well represented by Lucy Lippard's *The Lure of the Local: Senses of*

Place in a Multicentered Society. She presents a holistic vision of place as a kind of text of humanity, "the intersections of nature, culture, history, and ideology," that one understands as such from a position of an insider. Place, according to Lippard, is "a portion of land/town/cityscape seen from the inside, the resonance of a specific location that is known and familiar . . . 'the external world mediated through human subjective experience.' "[5] Lippard contends that since our sense of identity is fundamentally tied to our relationship to places and the histories they embody, the uprooting of our lives from specific local cultures and places—through voluntary migrations or forced displacements—has contributed to the waning of our abilities to locate ourselves. Consequently, a sense of place remains remote to most of us. And this deficiency can be seen as a primary cause of our loss of touch with nature, disconnection from history, spiritual vacancy, and estrangement from our own sense of self. She argues that we need to pay closer attention to the role of places in the formation of our identities and cultural values; and she encourages a particular type of relationship to places as a means of countering the trends of the dominant capitalist culture. Vaguely recalling Martin Heidegger's phenomenological philosophy on dwelling and place, which diagnosed the *modern* condition as one of an existential "homelessness" (according to the philosopher, the world hasn't been the "right place" for mankind for a very long time),[6] Lippard presents a sense of place as therapeutic remedy: sense of place is "the geographical component of the psychological need to belong somewhere, one antidote to a prevailing alienation."[7]

Even as she recalls some conservative aspects of Heidegger, or more accurately of his subsequent interpreters such as Yi-Tu Fuan[8] and Christian Norberg-Schulz,[9] Lippard also incorporates aspects of the Marxist analysis of the "production of space." She begins, for instance, from the basic premise that space is not a neutral container or void within which social interactions take place but rather an ideological product and instrument in itself. More specifically, she believes that the rapacious growth and transformation of capitalism have subsumed the distinctions of local differences and cultures, and that the particularity of places is continually being homogenized, genericized, and commodified to better accommodate the expansion of capitalism via abstraction of space (or creation of "nonplaces," as some sociologists prefer).[10] These processes, in turn, exasperate the sense of placelessness in contemporary life.

But unlike Lefebvre, who provides the deepest dialectical consideration of the "production of space" (his phrase), Lippard seems unable to resist the nostalgic impulse. In the end, the task of a progressive oppositional cultural practice is conceived as a retrieval and resuscitation of a lost sense of place. Her project implicitly calls for a slower, more sedentary mode of existence. Despite her disclaimers, hers is a vision that favors the "return" to a vernacular, nonurban sociality of small-scale spaces and face-to-face exchanges.[11] Not that such a vision isn't appealing. The problem may be that it is all too appealing, not only to us individually but to the machinations of capitalism itself.

What Lippard's thinking misses are Lefebvre's important insights on the *dialectical* rather than oppositional relationship between the increasing abstraction of space and the "production" of particularities of place, local specificity, and cultural authenticity—a concern that informs many site-oriented art practices today. Production of difference, to say it in more general terms, is itself a fundamental activity of capitalism, necessary for its continuous expansion. One might go so far as to say that this desire for difference, authenticity, and our willingness to pay high prices for it only highlight the degree to which they are already lost to us (thus the power they have over us).

A contrary position to Lippard's advocacy of place-bound identity celebrates the nomadic condition. Often leaning on Gilles Deleuze and Félix Guattari for theoretical support, some critics have championed the work of certain artists for having abandoned the phenomenologically oriented mode of site-specific art (best exemplified by Richard Serra's sculptures). Moving beyond the inherited conception of site-specific art as a grounded, fixed (even if ephemeral), singular event, the work of artists such as Andrea Fraser, Mark Dion, Renée Green, and Christian Philipp Müller, among many others, is seen to advance an altogether different notion of a site as predominantly an intertextually coordinated, multiply located, discursive field of operation.

This is the reading, for example, of James Meyer, who coined the term "functional site" to distinguish recent site-oriented practices from those of the past.[12] This conceptual shift has embraced the idea of meaning as an open, unfixed constellation, porous to contingencies—an idea that most of us accept and welcome. But in the process, the idea of the fluidity of meaning has tended to get conflated or confused with the idea of fluidity of identities and subjectivities, even of physical bodies, to such an extent that a certain romanticism has accrued around the image of the cultural worker on the go. Not only is the art work not bound to the physical conditions of a place anymore, but the artist-subject is "liberated" from any enduring ties to local circumstances. Qualities of permanence, continuity, certainty, groundedness (physical and otherwise) are thought to be artistically retrograde, thus politically suspect, in this context. By contrast, uncertainty, instability, ambiguity, and impermanence are taken as desired attributes of a vanguard, politically progressive artistic practice. But I remain unconvinced of the ways a model of meaning and interpretation is called forth to validate, even romanticize, the material and socioeconomic realities of an itinerant lifestyle. I am suspicious of this analogical transposition and the seductive allure of nomadism it supports, if for no other reason than the fact of my own personal ambivalence toward the physical and psychical experiences of mobilization and destabilization that such nomadism demands. To embrace such conditions is to leave oneself vulnerable to new terrors and dangers. At the very least, we have to acknowledge this vulnerability.[13]

I want to remember in this context a particular lesson of a "wrong" place described by novelist Don DeLillo in his recent two-act play *Valparaiso* (1999).[14] In the play, the protagonist, Michael Majeski, an average middle-class businessman (assumed to be white), on an ordinary business trip to Valparaiso, Indiana, ends up in another part of the world in Valparaiso, Chile, presumably by mistake, and then has to confront his own minor media celebrity on his return home. Majeski's extraordinary misadventure of falling off the track of his set itinerary and ending up in the wrong place (which isn't to say that he gets lost) is the starting point for DeLillo's fictional critique of the postmodern condition, in which the disruption of a subject's habitual spatiotemporal experience propels the liberation and also the breakdown of its traditional sense of self.

The play begins with Majeski recently returned from the unintended destination of his trip, the wrong Valparaiso in Chile (there are four Valparaisos in the world, so far as I am aware). Upon his return, he is confronted with numerous requests by the media—radio, television, newspapers, magazines, documentary filmmakers—to recount his experience. It is a great human interest story, after all: we all want to know what happened. How could anyone make such a big mistake? Didn't he notice that he was headed for the wrong city? When did he notice? Why was he going to Valparaiso in the first place? What happened exactly? Who is Michael Majeski? What was he like as a child? What are his dreams? Does he love his wife? Submitting to such questions, he does 67 interviews in four and a half days in three and a half cities (at least we are told so by his wife), forced to repeat his narrative over and over in front of microphones and cameras, simultaneously constructing and confessing his identity and life history, including his struggles with alcoholism and the drunken car accident that disabled his only son.

With most of the scenes set in talk show "living rooms," DeLillo's primary concern is clearly the omnipresence of broadcast technology as an organizing force in our lives and minds. Indeed the collapse of traditional spatial and temporal modalities, and the fragmentation, discontinuity, and intensities presented by new modalities, are conveyed by the characters primarily through their use of language. The dialogue is full of truncated hesitations, random misfires, incomplete thoughts, and broken repetitions, as if the characters aren't really speaking to one another but through and past each other. Their disjunctive conversations sound more like a set of uncoordinated soundtracks. Their words do not constitute even a monologue in that there are no real listeners, not even an inner self. Everyone speaks to, and answers to, an invisible ear, one that belongs to a phantom body of a televisual public.[15]

The fractured nature of DeLillo's language is not unlike that of Fredric Jameson's "schizophrenic" postmodern subject who, in the throes of an overwhelmingly intense or traumatic present, is unable to make coherent sense in any recognizable, conventional manner due to an utter breakdown of the basic temporality of narrative continuity.[16] But DeLillo's play has much to say on spatial issues, too, even if only implicitly. First, the space of our public conversations is now fully circumscribed by the camera or the media: life is footage waiting to be shot. Experience is not real unless it is recorded and validated through media representation. It is in this mediated virtual space that "we talk to each other today. This is the way we tell each other things, in public, before listening millions, that we don't dare to say privately."[17]

Secondly, spatial experience, like the broken temporality of language, is discontinuous and creepily disembodied. The words do not reach deep, they collage fleeting fragmentary impressions, and vision does not (cannot) distinguish between what is seen and the mediation of that scene. For example, Majeski describes the beginning of his journey to an interviewer: "I'm watching the takeoff on live video. I'm on the plane, I'm in my seat. There's a monitor on the bulkhead. I look at the monitor and the plane is taking off. I look out the window and the plane is taking off. Then what. The plane is taking off outside the cabin and the plane is taking off inside the cabin. I look at the monitor, I look at the earth."[18]

Thirdly, it is important to remember that the plot of the play is premised on an instance of locational misrecognition, on a character's temporarily losing his way in the world. How does this happen? Majeski leaves his house early in the morning to board a plane to Chicago. From there, he is to be picked up and driven to Valparaiso, Indiana, some forty miles away. But at the airport, the ticket counter attendant notices a discrepancy between his ticket (for Chicago) and his printed itinerary (for Miami). She tries to be helpful and finds him a seat on the Miami flight, about to take off; even though he was fully prepared for the Chicago flight, Majeski, not wanting to be discourteous to the attendant, makes a quick nondecision to head for Valparaiso, Florida, via Miami. Once in Miami, instead of boarding a chartered plane for this second Valparaiso, he somehow ends up on an international flight to Santiago, headed for Valparaiso, Chile. Details remain vague.

Majeski recalls the experience on a television talk show:

> Yes. It was strange. The aircraft seemed too big, too wide-bodied for an intrastate flight. . . . And I said nothing. I was intimidated by the

> systems. The enormous sense of power all around me. Heaving and breathing. How could I impose myself against this force? The electrical systems. The revving engines. . . . The sense of life support. The oxygen in the oxygen masks. . . . I felt submissive. I had to submit to the systems. They were all-powerful and all-knowing. If I was sitting in this assigned seat. Think about it. If the computers and metal detectors and uniformed personnel and bomb-sniffing dogs had allowed me to reach this assigned seat and given me this airline blanket that I could not rip out of its plastic shroud, then I must belong here. That's how I was thinking at the time.[19]

Majeski ends up in Chile not out of absentmindedness but because he recognizes a hitherto unknown logic of belonging, a sense of belonging that is not bound to any specific location but to a system of movement. Majeski does not resist the ways in which bodies are channeled through the sky along the prescribed trajectories of commercial air travel. He believes in its intimidating logic, has faith in its procedures, respects its timetables. He attributes almost mystical powers to the system. He might have ended up in the wrong city, but, in a sense, he was in the right place all along. So that when he reaches Santiago, fully aware of his mistake, it no longer matters how far he has strayed. He is calm. Instead of turning back, he is convinced to *complete* his mistake, to go all the way to Chile's Valparaiso. "For the beauty and balance. The formal resolution."[20] (Indeed, had Michael Majeski been an artist and his trip an art project, I would have been moved to think it a brilliant critique of site specificity.)

Often we are comforted by the thought that a place is ours, that we belong to it, even come from it, and therefore are tied to it in some fundamental way. Such places ("right" places?) are thought to reaffirm our sense of self, reflecting back to us an unthreatening picture of a grounded identity. This kind of continuous relationship between a place and a person is what many critics declare to be lost, and needed, in contemporary society. In contrast, the "wrong" place is generally thought of as a place where one feels one does not belong—unfamiliar, disorienting, destabilizing, even threatening. This kind of stressful relationship to a place is, in turn, thought to be detrimental to a subject's capacity to constitute a coherent sense of self and the world.

Thanks to the perfection and formal beauty of Majeski's mistake, we can think about the "wrong" place in altogether new ways. Rather than his "losing himself" because he ends up in the wrong place, quite the opposite seems to happen in *Valparaiso*. Finding himself in an airplane headed for the wrong city, Majeski begins to recognize himself, or more precisely the conditions of his own estrangement, and is set on a journey to account for his identity. In the telling and retelling of the tale, his rather tragic and fractured sense of self is revealed not only to us, the audience, but to the character himself. It is the wrongness rather than rightness of place that brings Majeski into focus. As the play progresses, it become less and less clear whether Majeski was trapped in a journey headed for the wrong place or the trip was in fact an attempt to *escape from* a wrong place—his home, his job, his marriage, his family, his life, himself. An encounter with a "wrong" place is likely to expose the instability of the "right" place, and by extension the instability of the self. The price of such awakening is steep, however, as the concluding scenes of the play reveal. Suffice it to say that Majeski's psychological unmooring as a result of his trip both liberates and shatters him.

* * *

It seems historically inevitable that we will leave behind the nostalgic notion of a site and identity as essentially bound to the physical actualities of a place. Such a notion, if not ideologically suspect, is at least out of sync with the prevalent description of contemporary life as a network of unanchored flows. Even an advanced theoretical position like Frampton's critical regionalism seems dated in this regard; for it is predicated on the belief that a particular site/place, with its identity-giving or identifying properties, exists always and already *prior* to whatever new cultural forms might be introduced to it or emerge from it. In such a pre- (or post-) post-structuralist conception, all site-specific gestures would have to be understood as reactive, cultivating what is presumed to be there already rather than generating new identities and histories.

Indeed, the deterritorialization of the site has produced liberating effects, displacing the strictures of place-bound identities with the fluidity of a migratory model, introducing possibilities for the production of multiple identities, allegiances, and meanings, based not on normative conformities but on the nonrational convergences forged by chance encounters and circumstances. The fluidity of subjectivity, identity, and spatiality as described by Deleuze and Guattari in their rhyzomatic nomadism,[21] for example, is a powerful theoretical tool for the dismantling of traditional orthodoxies that would suppress differences, sometimes violently.

Despite the proliferation of discursive sites and fictional selves, however, the phantom of a site as an actual place remains, and our psychic, habitual attachment to places regularly returns as it continues to inform our sense of identity. This persistent, perhaps secret adherence to the actuality of places (in memory, in longing) may not be a lack of theoretical sophistication but a means of survival. The resurgence of violence in defense of essentialized notions of national, racial, religious, and cultural identities in relation to geographical territories is readily characterized as extremist, retrograde, and uncivilized. Yet the loosening of such relations, that is, the destabilization of subjectivity, identity, and spatiality (following the dictates of desire), can also be described as a compensatory fantasy in response to the intensification of fragmentation and alienation wrought by a mobilized market economy (following the dictates of capital). The advocacy of the continuous mobilization of self- and place identities as discursive fictions, as polymorphous critical plays on fixed generalities and stereotypes, in the end may be a delusional alibi for short attention spans, reinforcing the ideology of the new—a temporary antidote for the anxiety of boredom. It is perhaps too soon and frightening to acknowledge, but the paradigm of nomadic selves and sites may be a glamorization of the trickster ethos that is in fact a reprise of the ideology of "freedom of choice"—the choice to forget, the choice to reinvent, the choice to fictionalize, the choice to "belong" anywhere, everywhere, and nowhere. This choice, of course, does not belong to everyone equally. The understanding of identity and difference as being culturally constructed should not obscure the fact that the ability to deploy multiple, fluid identities in and of itself is a privilege of mobility that has a specific relationship to power.

What would it mean now to sustain the cultural and historical specificity of a place (and self) that is neither a simulacral pacifier nor a willful invention? For architecture, Frampton proposes a process of "double mediation," which is in fact a double negation, *defying* "both the optimization of advanced technology and the ever-present tendency to regress into nostalgic historicism or the glibly decorative."[22] An analogous double mediation in site-specific art practice might mean finding a terrain between mobilization and specificity—to be *out* of place with punctuality and precision. Homi Bhabha has said, "The globe shrinks for those who own it; for the displaced or the dispossessed, the migrant or refugee, no distance is more awesome than the few feet across borders or frontiers."[23]

Thus, it is not a matter of choosing sides—between models of nomadism and sedentariness, between space and place, between digital interfaces and the handshake. Rather, we need to be able to think the range of the seeming contradictions and our contradictory desires for them together; to understand, in other words, seeming oppositions as *sustaining* relations. How do we account, for instance, for the sense of soaring exhilaration and the anxious dread engendered by the new fluidities and continuities of space and time, on the one hand, and their ruptures and disconnections on the other? And what could this doubleness of experience mean in our lives? in our work? Today's site-oriented practices inherit the task of demarcating the *relational specificity* that can hold in dialectical tension the distant poles of spatial experience described by Bhabha. This means addressing the uneven conditions of adjacencies and distances *between* one thing, one person, one place, one thought, one fragment *next* to another, rather than invoking equivalences via one thing *after* another. Only those cultural practices that have this relational sensibility can turn local encounters into long-term commitments and transform passing intimacies into indelible, unretractable social marks—so that the sequence of sites that we inhabit in our life's traversal does not become genericized into an undifferentiated serialization, one place after another.

Gabriel Orozco, ***Isla dentro de la isla (Island into the Island)***, 1992. (Courtesy Marian Goodman Gallery, New York.)

NOTES

INTRODUCTION

1 The two concurrent exhibitions organized in conjunction with the 1996 Olympic Games in Atlanta, Georgia, are good examples of the confusing uses of the term "site specificity" in contemporary art discourse. The exhibitions were "Rings," a thematic show structured around the "five universal emotions symbolically related to the number of the Olympic rings," and "Picturing the South: 1860 to the Present," a photography exhibition with a regional focus on the history and culture of the American South, especially Atlanta. In the press release for the exhibitions, Ned Rifkin, Director of the High Museum of Art in Atlanta, promoted the former rather than the latter as a site-specific exhibition. In this case, despite the universalizing theme of "Rings," its temporal coordination with the Olympic Games would seem to trump the geographical specificity of "Picturing the South."

2 These terms are used rather loosely and interchangeably in current art discourse. The concept of debate specificity, however, was coined in the 1970s by Mary Kelly to describe her move away from the prevailing dominance of concerns for medium specificity in art discourse. See her comments in her interview with Douglas Crimp in *Mary Kelly* (London: Phaidon Press, 1997), 15. Kelly's debate specificity corresponds to the notion of discursive sites that I develop in chapter 1.

3 In addition to a few articles, three recent books begin to address this problem: Julie H. Reiss, *From Margin to Center: The Spaces of Installation Art* (Cambridge: MIT Press, 1999); Nick Kaye, *Site-Specific Art: Performance, Place, and Documentation* (London: Routledge, 2000); and Erika Suderburg, ed., *Space, Site, Intervention: Situating Installation Art* (Minneapolis: University of Minnesota Press, 2000). Much work remains, however, in historicizing and theorizing site-specific art, as distinct from installation art.

4 I borrow this concept from William Pietz, who characterized the "fetish" as such a "problem-idea."

5 Rosalyn Deutsche, *Evictions: Art and Spatial Politics* (Cambridge: MIT Press, 1996), xi.

6 Ibid. See especially chapter two, "Uneven Development: Public Art in New York City."

7 The term is borrowed from Hal Foster's essay "The Un/making of Sculpture," in Russell Ferguson, Anthony McCall, and Clara Weyergraf-Serra, eds., *Richard Serra: Sculpture 1985–1998* (Los Angeles and Göttingen, Germany: Museum of Contemporary Art and Steidl Verlag, 1998).

8 See Suzanne Lacy, ed., *Mapping the Terrain: New Genre Public Art* (Seattle: Bay Press, 1995).

9 See Bruce Robbins, ed., *The Phantom Public Sphere* (Minneapolis: University of Minnesota Press, 1993).

10 Fredric Jameson, *Postmodernism, or, the Cultural Logic of Late Capitalism* (Durham: Duke University Press, 1991).

11 Lucy Lippard, *The Lure of the Local: Senses of Place in a Multicultural Society* (New York: New Press, 1997).

12 Kenneth Frampton, "Towards a Critical Regionalism," in Hal Foster, ed., *The Anti-Aesthetic: Essays on Postmodern Culture* (Port Townsend, Wash.: Bay Press, 1983).

13 Michel de Certeau, *The Practice of Everyday Life* (Minneapolis: University of Minnesota Press, 1984).

14 Henri Lefebvre, *The Production of Space,* trans. Donald Nicholson-Smith (1974; Oxford and Cambridge: Blackwell, 1991).

1

1 Douglas Crimp has written: "The idealism of modernist art, in which the art object *in and of itself* was seen to have a fixed and transhistorical meaning, determined the object's placelessness, its belonging in no particular place, a no-place that was in reality the museum. . . . Site specificity opposed that idealism—and unveiled the material system it obscured—by its refusal of circulatory mobility, its belongingness to a *specific* site." Douglas Crimp, *On the Museum's Ruins* (Cambridge: MIT Press, 1993), 17. See also Rosalind Krauss, "Sculpture in the Expanded Field" (1979), in Hal Foster, ed., *The Anti-Aesthetic: Essays on Postmodern Culture* (Port Townsend, Wash.: Bay Press, 1983), 31–42.

2 William Turner, British sculptor, as quoted by Mary Miss in "From Autocracy to Integration: Redefining the Objectives of Public Art," in Stacy Paleologos Harris, ed.,

Insights/On Sites: Perspectives on Art in Public Places (Washington, D.C.: Partners for Livable Places, 1984), 62.

3 Rosalyn Deutsche has made an important distinction between an assimilative model of site specificity—in which the art work is geared toward *integration* into the existing environment, producing a unified, "harmonious" space of wholeness and cohesion—and an interruptive model in which the art work functions as a critical *intervention* in the existing order of a site through some sort of disruption. See her essays "*Tilted Arc* and the Uses of Public Space," *Design Book Review* 23 (Winter 1992): 22–27; and "Uneven Development: Public Art in New York City," *October* 47 (Winter 1988): 3–52. For more on this distinction in the context of public art, see chapter 3.

4 Michael Fried, "Art and Objecthood" (1967), in Gregory Battcock, ed., *Minimal Art: A Critical Anthology* (New York: Dutton, 1968), 116–147.

5 Robert Barry in Arthur R. Rose (pseud.), "Four Interviews with Barry, Huebler, Kosuth, Weiner," *Arts Magazine* (February 1969): 22.

6 Richard Serra, letter to Donald Thalacker dated January 1, 1985, as published in Clara Weyergraf-Serra and Martha Buskirk, eds., *The Destruction of Tilted Arc: Documents* (Cambridge: MIT Press, 1991), 38. See chapter 3 for more on the *Tilted Arc* controversy.

7 Richard Serra, "*Tilted Arc* Destroyed," *Art in America* 77, no. 5 (May 1989): 34–47.

8 The controversy over *Tilted Arc* obviously involved other issues besides the status of site specificity, but, in the end, site specificity was the term upon which Serra hung his entire defense. Despite his defeat, the legal definition of site specificity still remains unresolved and continues to be grounds for many juridical conflicts. For a discussion concerning legal questions in the *Tilted Arc* case, see Barbara Hoffman, "Law for Art's Sake in the Public Realm," in W. J. T. Mitchell, ed., *Art in the Public Sphere* (Chicago: University of Chicago Press, 1991), 113–146. Thanks to James Marcovitz for discussions concerning the legality of site specificity.

9 See Hal Foster's seminal essay "The Crux of Minimalism," in Howard Singerman, ed., *Individuals: A Selected History of Contemporary Art 1945–1986* (Los Angeles: Museum of Contemporary Art, 1986), 162–183. See also Craig Owens, "From Work to Frame, or, Is There Life After 'The Death of the Author'?," in Scott Bryson et al., eds., *Beyond Recognition: Representation, Power, and Culture* (Berkeley: University of California Press, 1992), 122–139.

10 Daniel Buren, "The Function of the Museum," *Artforum* (September 1973).

11 Daniel Buren, "Critical Limits" (1970), in *Five Texts* (New York: John Weber Gallery, 1974), 38.

12 See "Conversation with Robert Smithson," edited by Bruce Kurtz, in *The Writings of Robert Smithson,* ed. Nancy Holt (New York: New York University Press, 1979), 200.

13 For a comprehensive overview of Haacke's practice from 1969 to 1986, see *Hans Haacke: Unfinished Business,* ed. Brian Wallis (New York and Cambridge: New Museum of Contemporary Art and MIT Press, 1986).

14 This project involved the relocation of a bronze replica of an eighteenth-century statue of George Washington from its normal position outside the entrance of the Art Institute to one of the smaller galleries inside devoted to eighteenth-century European painting, sculpture, and decorative arts. Asher stated his intentions as follows: "In this work I am interested in the way the sculpture functions when it is viewed in its 18th-century context instead of in its prior relationship to the façade of the building. . . . Once inside Gallery 219 the sculpture can be seen in connection with the ideas of other European works of the same period" (as quoted in Anne Rorimer, "Michael Asher: Recent Work," *Artforum* [April 1980]: 47). See also Benjamin Buchloh, ed., *Michael Asher: Writings 1973–1983 on Works 1969–1979* (Halifax, Nova Scotia, and Los Angeles: Press of the Nova Scotia College of Art and Design and Museum of Contemporary Art, Los Angeles), 207–221.

15 The four performances at the Wadsworth Atheneum, which belong to a larger series (fifteen in all) entitled *Maintenance Art Performance Series* (1973–1974), were in the context of the exhibition "c. 7,500," a traveling exhibition of works by twenty-six women conceptual artists organized by Lucy Lippard. Unfortunately, information on the work of women artists of the period involved in conceptual art, institutional critique, and social systems analysis, like Ukeles, remains obscure due to their continued exclusion from the dominant art historical narratives of the 1970s. The few source materials that are available on Ukeles's work tend to be fraught with factual errors. For instance, Ukeles's "Maintenance Art Manifesto" (1969), as published in Kristine Stiles and Peter Selz, eds., *Theories and Documents of Contemporary Art: A Sourcebook of Artists' Writings* (Berkeley: University of California Press, 1996), is not only incomplete in its truncation of the statement but has been edited so as to render it useless as a historical document. An effort has been initiated to recuperate some of Ukeles's earlier work. See *Documents* 10 (Fall 1997): 5–30. I also refer the readers to Patricia Phillips, "Maintenance Activity:

Creating a Climate of Change," in Nina Felshin, ed., *But Is It Art?: The Spirit of Art as Activism* (Seattle: Bay Press, 1995), 165–194, for a brief survey on the artist's history and work.

16 For an elaboration on these points, see my essay "In Appreciation of Invisible Work: Mierle Laderman Ukeles and the Maintenance of the 'White Cube,'" *Documents* 10 (Fall 1997): 15–18. See also Helen Molesworth, "Work Stoppages: Mierle Laderman Ukeles' Theory of Labor Value," *Documents* 10 (Fall 1997): 19–22; and "House Work and Art Work," *October* 92 (Spring 2000): 71–97, which asserts a set of new terms, via Ukeles's "maintenance art," for the reconsideration of the history of feminist art since the 1970s.

17 This is not to say that art is not already imbricated within the social. But much of the discourse I am describing imagines the social as a space separate from, indeed antithetical to, the space of art, and that is what I mean to convey here.

18 These concerns coincide with developments in public art, which has reprogrammed site-specific art to be synonymous with community-based art. As exemplified in programs such as "Culture in Action" in Chicago (1992–1993) and "Points of Entry" in Pittsburgh (1996), site-specific public art in the 1990s marks a convergence between cultural practices grounded in leftist political activism, community-based aesthetic traditions, conceptually driven art borne out of institutional critique, and identity politics. An interrogation of site specificity in the public art arena is the subject of chapters 3 and 4. See also Grant Kester's excellent analysis of recent trends in community-based public art in "Aesthetic Evangelists: Conversion and Empowerment in Contemporary Community Art," *Afterimage* (January 1995): 5–11.

19 The exhibition "Arte Joven en Nueva York" was curated by artist José Gabriel Fernandez and hosted by Sala Mendoza and Sala RG in Caracas, Venezuela (June 9–July 7, 1991).

20 This fourth site, to which Dion would return again and again in other projects, remained consistent even as the contents of one of the crates from the Orinoco trip were transferred to New York City to be reconfigured in 1992 to become *New York State Bureau of Tropical Conservation,* an installation for an exhibition at American Fine Arts, Co. See the conversation "The Confessions of an Amateur Naturalist," *Documents* 1–2 (Fall/Winter 1992): 36–46. See also my interview with Dion in the monograph *Mark Dion* (London: Phaidon Press, 1997).

21 For additional information on the works I have in mind, see chapter 2, note 25 for Silvia

Kolbowski; and chapter 5, note 31 for Group Material. For relevant writings on Christian Philipp Müller, see George Baker, "Lies, Damn Lies, and Statistics: The Art of Christian Philipp Müller," *Artforum* (February 1997): 74–77, and "A Balancing Act," *October* 82 (Fall 1997): 94–118; James Meyer, "Nomads," *Parkett* 35 (May 1997): 205–214; and Christian Philipp Müller, *Branding the Campus: Art, Architecture, Design, Politics of Identity* (Düsseldorf: Richter Verlag, 2001).

22 See the roundtable discussion "On Site Specificity," in *Documents* 4–5 (Spring 1994): 11–22. Participants included Hal Foster, Renée Green, Mitchell Kane, John Lindell, Helen Molesworth, and myself.

23 James Meyer, "The Functional Site," in *Platzwechsel*, exh. cat. (Zurich: Kunsthalle Zürich, 1995): 27. A revised version of the essay appears in *Documents* 7 (Fall 1996): 20–29. Meyer's theorization of the development of site specificity is indebted, as mine is, to the historical and theoretical work of Craig Owens, Rosalind Krauss, Douglas Crimp, Hal Foster, and Benjamin Buchloh, among others. While I concur generally with Meyer's description of recent site-oriented art, our interpretations lead to different questions and conclusions, as will be evident in this and subsequent chapters.

24 Despite the adoption of architectural terminology in the description of many new electronic spaces (websites, information environments, programming infrastructures, construction of home pages, virtual spaces, etc.), the spatial experience on the computer is structured more as a sequence of movements and passages than as the habitation or durational occupation of a particular "site." Hypertext is a prime example. The (information) superhighway is a more apt analogy, for the spatial experience of the highway is one of transit between locations (despite one's immobile body behind the wheel).

25 Again, these concerns overlap with discussions in the public art field. See chapters 3 and 4. Regarding the "public" status of contemporary art, see Rosalyn Deutsche, *Evictions: Art and Spatial Politics* (Cambridge: MIT Press, 1996).

26 For example, see Gilles Deleuze, "Postscript on the Societies of Control," *October* 59 (Winter 1992): 3–7; and Manuel Castells, *The Informational City* (Oxford: Basil Blackwell, 1989).

2

1 For an overview of this situation, see Susan Hapgood, "Remaking Art History," *Art in America* (July 1990): 115–123, 181.

2 "The New Sculpture 1965–75: Between Geometry and Gesture" at the Whitney Museum (1990) included fourteen recreations of works by Barry Le Va, Bruce Nauman, Alan Saret, Richard Serra, Joel Shapiro, Keith Sonnier, and Richard Tuttle. Le Va's recreation of *Continuous and Related Activities: Discontinued by the Act of Dropping* from 1967 was then purchased by the Whitney Museum for its permanent collection and subsequently reinstalled in several other exhibitions, "traveling" to many different locations. The exhibition as a whole traveled to the Museum of Contemporary Art Los Angeles later the same year.

3 Mel Bochner, in a 1969 interview with Elayne Varian, proposed a way of thinking about repetition and portability of art in light of his *Measurement* series, in which there is no conclusive original, thus no copies. "The piece could be in my studio, and in someone's collection, and in an exhibition simultaneously. It doesn't come down in one place and go up in another. In this sense the piece is not a portable object, it's a portable idea. As long as the internal relationships of measurements and materials remain constant it's the same work no matter where it is." Such a comment signals the need to distinguish between works that are physically and conceptually site-specific and those that are site-dependent but conceptually independent. See Elayne Varian, "An Interview with Mel Bochner" (1969), *Documents* 20 (Spring 2001): 4–8. See also Miwon Kwon, "Portable Ideas: An Interview with Mel Bochner," in the same issue.

4 Hapgood, "Remaking Art History," 120.

5 This was the logic behind Richard Serra's defense of *Tilted Arc*. Consequently, the issue of relocation or removal of the sculpture became a debate concerning the creative rights of the artist. For more on *Tilted Arc*, see chapter 3.

6 On the exhibition, entitled "Innovations: Entering into the Sculpture" (October 10–November 25, 1989), see Frances Colpitt, "Report from Los Angeles: Space Invaders," *Art in America* (January 1990): 67–71. In Carl Andre's letter to the editor (*Art in America* [March 1990]: 31), he notes that he only became aware of the Ace Gallery exhibition as a result of Colpitt's article. Donald Judd similarly remarks on the accidental nature of his finding out about the duplication of his work. See his letter to the editor, "Artist Disowns 'Copied' Sculpture," *Art in America* (April 1990): 33.

7 For Count Giuseppe Panza's thoughts on the original installation of these two works, see his interview with Christopher Knight in *Art of the Fifties, Sixties and Seventies: The Panza Collection* (Milan: Editoriale Jaca Books, 1999).

8 Sol LeWitt seems to have understood this shift quite early in his career. Like many of his mini-

mal art colleagues, he used fabricators to produce his serial objects in the mid-1960s. But when he began using "surrogate" producers for his wall drawings in the late 1960s, which became a necessity as the scale and demand for such work increased through the 1970s, he formally adopted the practice of providing certificates of authenticity along with diagrammed instructions for the making of the drawings; these instructions were taken as, or at least comparable to, the art work. The authenticity of a LeWitt wall drawing, thus, was no longer predicated on who actually made the drawing but on the verification provided by the artist in the form of *signed* instructions. Although he has altered his view in recent years, he once believed that anyone could make a Sol LeWitt wall work if the person followed his instructions precisely. Divergent strategies along these lines were adopted by other artists of the period, including Dan Flavin, Douglas Huebler, Robert Barry, and Lawrence Weiner. The significance of the function of the artist's signature, of course, was highlighted many decades earlier by Marcel Duchamp. Some of Piero Manzoni's work from the early 1960s, such as the signing of certain persons to designate them as works of art, also serves as an important precursor to the consideration of the primacy of the artist's signature in the art of the 1970s.

9 See Rosalind Krauss, "The Cultural Logic of the Late Capitalist Museum," *October* 54 (Fall 1990): 3–17.

10 For Wilding's description of this dilemma, as well as her assessment of recent revisits of 1960s and 1970s feminist art, see her essay "Monstrous Domesticity," in *M/E/A/N/I/N/G* 18 (November 1995): 3–16. On Womanhouse and the Feminist Art Program at the California Institute of the Arts, see Wilding, "The Feminist Art Programs at Fresno and CalArts, 1970–75," and Arlene Raven, "Womanhouse," in Norma Broude and Mary D. Garrard, eds., *The Power of Feminist Art: The American Movement of the 1970s, History and Impact* (New York: Harry N. Abrams, 1994).

11 See Hal Foster, "The Artist as Ethnographer," in *The Return of the Real: The Avant-Garde at the End of the Century* (Cambridge: MIT Press, 1996), on the complex exchange between art and anthropology in recent art.

12 Not exactly the portable studio or Marcel Duchamp's *Boîte-en-valise* (1941) but a descendant nonetheless. A productionist reading of modern art has focused on the model of the alienated and fragmentary labor of the assembly line worker as producer of objects. What I am proposing here is a consideration of another neglected model of labor, that of the itinerant salesman who, rather than being bound to a stationary point in the space of production, must travel extensively for the dissemination, distribution, and promotion of commodities.

13 The current modes of site-oriented practices can be mapped along an alternative genealogy

of performance art. Consider, for example, Vito Acconci's comments on performance art as a publicity-oriented, contract-based practice: "On the one hand, performance imposed the unsaleable onto the store that the gallery is. On the other hand, performance built that store up and confirmed the market-system: It increased the gallery's sales by acting as window-dressing and by providing publicity. . . . There was one way I loved to say the word 'performance,' one meaning of the world [sic] 'performance' I was committed to: 'Performance' in the sense of performing a contract—you promised you would do something, now you have to carry that promise out, bring that promise through to completion." Vito Acconci, "Performance after the Fact," *New Observations* 95 (May-June 1993): 29. Thanks to Frazer Ward for directing my attention to this text. For a recent consideration of site-specific art from the point of view of performance, see Nick Kaye, *Site-Specific Art: Performance, Place, and Documentation* (London: Routledge, 2000).

14 By strategically introducing objects from the material history of African Americans and Native Americans (until then buried in the Society's storage) into existing displays of refined cultural artifacts, Wilson exposed the extent to which the histories of these "minority" cultures have consistently been repressed in the dominant narrative of the history of the United States. The matter-of-fact juxtaposition of, for example, slave shackles from before the Civil War and elaborately decorated silver tea services from the same period, presented with equal distinction under the category of "Metal Works," provided disturbing visual evidence of the violent legacy of slavery and racism in this country. The project also served as a local critique of the Maryland Historical Society itself—Society's own holdings used to point up the prejudicial and exclusive nature of "definitive" museological histories written in the form of the institution's exhibitions and publications. For details on this project, see Lisa Corrin, ed., *Mining the Museum* (New York: New Press, 1994).

15 See Fred Wilson's interview with Martha Buskirk in *October* 70 (Fall 1994): 109–112.

16 In the name of interdisciplinarity, and in an effort to rejuvenate permanent collection exhibitions, several museums have also engaged high-profile philosophers, cultural theorists, sociologists, and other intellectuals from nonart fields for curatorial commissions. See, for instance, Jacques Derrida's curatorial project at the Louvre presented in the Hall Napoléon from October 26, 1990, to January 21, 1991, published as *Mémoires d'aveugle: L'autoportrait et autres ruines* (Paris: Editions de la Réunion des musées nationaux, 1990).

17 Isabelle Graw, "Field Work," *Flash Art* (November/December 1990): 137. Her observation here is in relation to Hans Haacke's practice but is relevant as a general statement concerning the current status of institutional critique. See also Frazer Ward, "The Haunted Museum: Institutional Critique and Publicity," *October* 73 (Summer 1995): 71–90.

18 See J. I. Gershuny and I. D. Miles, *The New Service Economy* (New York: Praeger, 1983); and Saskia Sassen, *The Global City: New York, London, Tokyo* (Princeton: Princeton University Press, 1991).

19 It should be noted that the artist herself initiated the project by offering such services through her "Prospectus for Corporations." See Fraser's *Report* (Vienna: EA-Generali Foundation, 1995). For a more general consideration of artistic practice as cultural service provision, see Andrea Fraser, "What's Intangible, Transitory, Mediating, Participatory, and Rendered in the Public Sphere?," *October* 80 (Spring 1997): 111–116. Proceedings of working-group discussions organized by Fraser and Helmut Draxler in 1993 around the theme of services, to which Fraser's text provides an introduction, are also of interest and appear in the same issue of *October.* See also Beatrice von Bismark, Diethelm Stoller, and Ulf Wuggenig, eds., *Games, Fights, Collaborations* (Stuttgart: Cantz Verlag, 1996).

20 Richard Serra, "Verb List, 1967–68," in *Writings Interviews* (Chicago: University of Chicago Press, 1994), 3.

21 Benjamin Buchloh, "Conceptual Art 1962–1969: From the Aesthetics of Administration to the Critique of Institutions," *October* 55 (Winter 1991): 105–143.

22 For instance, the "Views from Abroad" exhibition series at the Whitney Museum, which foregrounds "artistic" visions of European curators, is structured very much like site-specific commissions of artists that focus on museum permanent collections as described above. The first two exhibitions in the series featured the "visions" of Rudi Fuchs of the Stedelijk Museum, Amsterdam (June 29–October 1, 1995), and Jean-Christophe Ammann of the Museum für moderne Kunst, Frankfurt am Main (October 18, 1996–January 5, 1997). These exhibitions traveled to the curators' respective home institutions after their run in New York City.

23 According to James Meyer, a site-oriented practice based on a functional notion of a site "traces the *artist's* movements through and around the institution" and "reflect[s] the specific interests, educations, and formal decisions of the producer"; and "in the process of deferral, a signifying chain that traverses physical and discursive borders," the functional site "incorporates the body of the artist" (emphasis added). See Meyer, "The Functional Site," in *Platzwechsel*, exh. cat. (Zurich: Kunsthalle Zürich, 1995), 29, 33, 31, 35.

24 The installation consisted of *Bequest,* commissioned by the Worcester Art Museum in Massachusetts in 1991; *Import/Export Funk Office,* originally shown at the Christian Nagel Gallery in Cologne in 1992 and then reinstalled at the 1993 Biennial at the Whitney Museum

of American Art; *Mise en Scène,* first presented in 1992 in Clisson, France; and *Idyll Pursuits,* produced for a group exhibition in 1991 in Caracas, Venezuela. As a whole, *World Tour* was exhibited at the Museum of Contemporary Art, Los Angeles, in 1993, then traveled to the Dallas Museum of Art later the same year. See Russell Ferguson, ed., *World Tour,* exh. cat. (Los Angeles: Museum of Contemporary Art, 1993).

25 This is a project not exclusive to Green. Silvia Kolbowski, for instance, has proposed the coupling of generic sites and specific transferability in projects such as "Enlarged from the Catalogue: *The United States of America*" (1988). See the project annotations and Johanne Lamoureux's essay, "The Open Window Case: New Displays for an Old Western Paradigm," in *Silvia Kolbowski: XI Projects* (New York: Border Editions, 1993), 34–51, 6–15. There is a correspondence between Kolbowski's idea and Mel Bochner's remarks as cited in note 3 above.

26 This faith in the authenticity of place is evident in a wide range of disciplines. In urban studies, see Dolores Hayden, *The Power of Place: Urban Landscapes as Public History* (Cambridge: MIT Press, 1995). In cultural geography, see Michael Hough, *Out of Place: Restoring Identity to the Regional Landscape* (New Haven: Yale University Press, 1990). In philosophy, see Edward Casey, *The Fate of Place: A Philosophical History* (Berkeley: University of California Press, 1997). In relation to public art, see Ronald Lee Fleming and Renata von Tscharner, *PlaceMakers: Creating Public Art That Tells You Where You Are* (Boston, San Diego, and New York: Harcourt Brace Jovanovich, 1981). See also Lucy Lippard, *The Lure of the Local: The Sense of Place in a Multicultural Society* (New York: New Press, 1997). See chapter 6 for more on this issue.

27 *Places with a Past: New Site-Specific Art at Charleston's Spoleto Festival,* exh. cat. (New York: Rizzoli, 1991), 19. The exhibition took place May 24–August 4, 1991, with site-specific works by eighteen artists including Ann Hamilton, Christian Boltanski, Cindy Sherman, David Hammons, Lorna Simpson and Alva Rogers, Kate Ericson and Mel Ziegler, and Ronald Jones.

28 Precedents for "Places with a Past," in which the city as a whole becomes the exhibition site, include the Spoleto Festival in Italy (1962), "Skulptur Projekte" in Münster, Germany (1987), "The New Urban Landscape" in New York City (1988), and "Die Endlichkeit der Freiheit" in Berlin (1990).

29 Mary Jane Jacob, in *Places with a Past,* 17.

30 Ibid., 15.

31 Undated press release of 1997. Thus, programs like "Places with a Past" and "Sculpture.

Projects" share a similar investment in generating a sense of uniqueness and authenticity for their respective places of presentation. As such endeavors to engage art in the nurturing of specificities of locational difference gather momentum, there is a greater urgency in distinguishing between the *cultivation* of art and places and their *appropriation* for the promotion of cities as cultural commodities.

32 Kevin Robins, "Prisoners of the City: Whatever Can a Postmodern City Be?," in Erica Carter, James Donald, and Judith Squires, eds., *Space and Place: Theories of Identity and Location* (London: Lawrence & Wishart, 1993), 306.

33 Cultural critic Sharon Zukin has noted, "It seemed to be official policy [by the 1990s] that making a place for art in the city went along with establishing a marketable identity for the city as a whole." See Sharon Zukin, *The Culture of Cities* (Cambridge, Mass.: Blackwell Publishers, 1995), 23.

34 Addressing Robert Smithson's *Spiral Jetty* and the *Partially Buried Woodshed,* Craig Owens has made an important connection between melancholia and the redemptive logic of site specificity in "The Allegorical Impulse: Toward a Theory of Postmodernism," *October* 12 (Spring 1980): 67–86.

35 Thierry de Duve, "Ex Situ," *Art & Design* 8, no. 5–6 (May-June 1993): 25.

3

1 According to Ahearn (verified through the Alexander and Bonin Gallery, New York, May 2000), he has a "gentleman's agreement" with the city of New York that some day, when the funds become available through the sale of the original three sculptures, he will be given the opportunity to complete the project. How this completion will be pursued remains unclear. The original design of the traffic triangle was in collaboration with Nancy Owens, a landscape architect with the city's Parks Department.

2 All art is engaged in public discourse in one way or another; by "mainstream public art" I mean the specific category of art that is typically sponsored and/or administered by city, state, or national government agencies, in whole or in part. It involves bureaucratized review and approval procedures that are outside the museum or gallery system and often engage numerous nonart organizations, including local community groups, private foundations, and corporations. However, this chapter's limited working definition of the term is provisional, insofar as the meaning of the "public" in public art continues to be open to debate.

3 For background information on public art in the United States since the early 1960s, see John Beardsley, *Art in Public Places: A Survey of Community Sponsored Projects Supported by the NEA* (Washington, D.C.: Partners for Livable Places, 1981); Donald Thalacker, *The Place of Art in the World of Architecture* (New York: Chelsea House Publishers, 1980); and Harriet Senie, *Contemporary Public Sculpture: Tradition, Transformation, and Controversy* (New York: Oxford University Press, 1992).

4 See Arlene Raven, ed., *Art in the Public Interest* (New York: Da Capo Press, 1989); and Suzanne Lacy, ed., *Mapping the Terrain: New Genre Public Art* (Seattle: Bay Press, 1995).

5 The paradigm shifts I note here are further elaborated in my essay "For Hamburg: Public Art and Urban Identities," in *Kunst auf Schritt und Tritt* (*Public Art Is Everywhere*) (Hamburg, Germany: Kellner, 1997), 95–107.

6 In the mid-1970s, the phrase "art in public places" was used by some public art professionals to distinguish location-conscious art from "public art," sculptures that were simply placed in public spaces, like Calder's. Thus my use of "art in public places" to designate the latter may be confusing to some, but since the NEA used the phrase as the title of its own program to promote this type of art, I am adopting it here.

7 Interestingly, for Robert Morris the size and scale of a sculpture was directly proportional to its publicness: the smaller the work, the greater the demand for intimacy of perception (private); the larger the work, the greater the demand for a "public" interaction. See his "Notes on Sculpture," in Gregory Battcock, ed., *Minimal Art: A Critical Anthology* (New York: Dutton, 1968), 222–228.

8 Henry Moore, as quoted in Henry J. Seldis, *Henry Moore in America* (New York: Praeger, 1973), 176–177.

9 Ibid., 14–15.

10 There is an important distinction to be drawn between the GSA and the NEA: the former administers federally sponsored commissions; the latter administers "community"-initiated projects. Starting in 1963, the GSA mandated that 0.5 to 1 percent of the estimated construction costs of all new federal buildings be set aside for art. Local Percent for Art programs, which follow the GSA model, were first instituted in cities like Philadelphia, Baltimore, and Seattle in the early to mid 1960s. The NEA program, by contrast, was set up to respond to local initiatives (from ad hoc citizens' groups and not-for-profit institutions or organizations, like arts commissions). Once it accepts a proposal, the NEA offers a matching grant and,

through a small committee of art experts, helps administer the process of selecting a site, choosing and negotiating with an artist, arranging for transportation and installation of the work, and mounting educational efforts to introduce the artist's work to the local community. In many instances, those at the NEA advise on GSA commissions. See Beardsley, *Art in Public Places,* for more details.

11 The Livable Cities Program initiated by the NEA in 1977 as part of its architecture program, for example, explicitly sought to find "creativity and imagination—to get it from the artist and apply it to the problems of the built environment" so as to "give promise of economic and social benefit to the community." See Louis G. Redstone, with Ruth R. Redstone, *Public Art: New Directions* (New York: McGraw-Hill, 1981), vi.

12 In the eyes of the urban elite and city managers during the 1970s and 1980s, public art was also supposed to attract tourism, new businesses and work forces, and residential development, and was expected to boost a city's sense of identity. Public art initiatives since the 1960s, in fact, have always been tied to urban renewal and economic revitalization efforts. On these issues, see Kate Linker, "Public Sculpture: The Pursuit of the Pleasurable and Profitable Paradise," *Artforum* (March 1981): 64–73, and "Public Sculpture II: Provisions for the Paradise," *Artforum* (Summer 1981): 37–42. See also Sharon Zukin, *The Culture of Cities* (Cambridge, Mass.: Blackwell, 1995); Erika Doss, *Spirit Poles and Flying Pigs: Public Art and Cultural Democracy in American Communities* (Washington: Smithsonian Institution Press, 1995), especially chapter three, "Public Art in the Corporate Sphere"; and my essay "For Hamburg: Public Art and Urban Identities."

13 Sam Hunter, "The Public Agency as Patron," in *Art for the Public: The Collection of the Port Authority of New York and New Jersey* (New York: Port Authority of New York and New Jersey, 1985), 35.

14 In addition to Kate Linker's criticism, see also Lawrence Alloway, "The Public Sculpture Problem," *Studio International* 184 (October 1972): 123–124; and Alloway, "Problems of Iconography and Style," in *Urban Encounters: Art Architecture Audience,* exh. cat. (Philadelphia: Institute of Contemporary Art, University of Pennsylvania, 1980), 15–20.

15 According to Kate Linker, in the 1960s a large portion of funding for public art was provided by the private sector. Corporations sponsored art to adorn office buildings, shopping malls, banks, etc., creating a new kind of "public" space (privately owned, publicly accessible) that became available to art. A traditional nationalist ideology of older forms of public art was replaced by a business ideology, and modern, abstract, often large-scale sculptures predominated as a favored style. See Linker, "Public Sculpture."

16 The term is commonly attributed to architect James Wines of SITE. He is also known to have coined the phrase "turds on the plaza" to describe the ubiquitous abstract modernist sculptures on urban plazas.

17 Statement taken from the official Art-in-Public-Places grant application guidelines of the Visual Arts Program of the National Endowment for the Arts, as cited by Mary Jane Jacob in her essay "Outside the Loop," in *Culture in Action,* exh. cat. (Seattle: Bay Press, 1995), 54.

18 A brief history of this transition is recounted in Lacy, ed., *Mapping the Terrain,* 21–24. See also Richard Andrews, "Artists and the Visual Definition of Cities: The Experience of Seattle," in Stacy Paleologos Harris, ed., *Insights/On Sites: Perspectives on Art in Public Places* (Washington, D.C.: Partners for Livable Places, 1984), 16–23.

19 According to Richard Andrews, who headed Seattle's Percent for Art program during the 1970s, public art, from an arts agency point of view, can be divided into two distinct types: those works aligned with the tradition of *collecting*, which are object-oriented and site-transferable; and those that fall within the tradition of *building,* which are involved in the designing process of public buildings and places. The scale tipped toward site-integrated and immovable works beginning in the late 1970s. See Andrews, "Artists and the Visual Definition of Cities," 19.

20 Janet Kardon, "Street Wise/Street Foolish," in *Urban Encounters,* exh. cat., 8. The exhibition, featuring documentation of projects by artists, architects, and landscape architects, was held between March 19 and April 30, 1980.

21 Nancy Foote, "Sightings on Siting," in *Urban Encounters,* 25–34.

22 Linker sees an intimation of a solution in Robert Morris's landscape work *Grand Rapids Project* (1973–1974) in the way durational bodily experience of a particular spatial situation defines the work. See her concluding comments in "Public Sculpture," 70–73. See also Alloway, "Problems of Iconography and Style."

23 I am recalling here the distinction made by Rosalyn Deutsche between integrationist and interventionist approaches to site-specific art. In Deutsche's view, the former seeks to erase visible signs of social problems that might contradict the ideology of unity; the latter seeks to expose them. See her *Evictions: Art and Spatial Politics* (Cambridge: MIT Press, 1996), especially the chapters "Uneven Development" and "*Tilted Arc* and the Uses of Democracy."

24 From the official Art-in-Public-Places grant application guidelines of the Visual Arts Program

of the National Endowment for the Arts, as cited by Jacob, "Outside the Loop," 54.

25 This design team model of public art was more an ideal than a reality. Even in the most successful cases, the conventional hierarchy of roles was maintained; that is, the architect assumed leadership and dictated the parameters of the artist's contribution. Part of the problem remains the established patterns of building design and construction. On the benefits and problems of artist-architect design team collaborations, see Donna Graves, "Sharing Space: Some Observations on the Recent History and Possible Future of Public Art Collaborations," *Public Art Review* (Spring/Summer 1993): 10–13; Joan Marter, "Collaborations: Artists and Architects on Public Sites," *Art Journal* (Winter 1989): 315–320; Diane Shamash, "The A Team, Artists and Architects: Can They Work Together?," *Stroll: The Magazine of Outdoor Art and Street Culture* 6–7 (June 1988): 60–63. An exemplary project following this design team model is the Viewland/Hoffman Substation (1979) in Seattle by Andrew Keating, Sherry Markovitz, Lewis Simpson, artists, and Hobbs/Fukui, architects (commissioned by Seattle Arts Commission and Seattle City Light). For another interesting case study, see Steve Rosenthal, *Artists and Architects Collaborate: Designing the Wiesner Building* (Cambridge, Mass.: MIT Committee on the Visual Arts, 1985).

Siah Armajani has commented with dismay on the design team initiative, in which he participated numerous times: "Public art was a promise that became a nightmare. . . . In the first place, the idea of a design team just doesn't work . . . the kind of design team that just gets together around a table is like a situation comedy. It is cynical and unproductive. Genuine debate can't take place around a table in that way. You get what the real-estate developer and the arts administrator want because they control the money. The whole emphasis in most of these projects is on who can get along best with the others involved—at the expense of vision and fresh thinking." From Calvin Tompkins, "Open, Available, Useful," *New Yorker* (March 19, 1990): 71.

26 Deutsche, *Evictions,* 65. Deutsche has provided the most thorough analysis of the universalizing logic of beauty and utility at the basis of public art discourse, which has supported urban redevelopment and gentrification projects. Some public art professionals within the field also recognized early the potential problems with such utilitarianism. For instance, Richard Andrews wrote in 1984, "There is a danger in perceiving contextual projects as a panacea for public art—as a means to reduce controversy and make art 'useful.' . . . Legitimate concern exists that function should not become the primary criteria for an institutionalized program of public art. In Seattle we may provide funding for the First Avenue Street project of [Lewis "Buster"] Simpson and [Jack] Mackie, but we would be ill-advised to generate a 'street improvement program' of benches, light poles, and so on for all artists." Andrews, "Artists and the Visual Definition of Cities," 26.

27 For instance, Burton, arguably the most prominent and vocal among artists who espoused this utilitarianism in public art, once said of his street tables and seating design for the Equitable Assurance Building in New York City: "The social questions interest me more than the art ones. . . . Communal social values are now more important. What office workers do in their lunch hour is more important than my pushing the limits of my self-expression." As quoted in Douglas C. McGill, "Sculpture Goes Public," *New York Times Magazine* (April 27, 1986): 67.

28 Such practices are predicated on the conception of the site of art as mobilized and unfixed. As such, the site is not only a venue of presentation but constitutes a mode of distribution as well. I have described this kind of deterritorialized site as a "discursive site." See chapter 1.

29 Richard Serra, "Rigging," interview with Gerard Hovagymyan, in *Richard Serra: Interviews, Etc. 1970–1980* (Yonkers, N.Y.: Hudson River Museum, 1980), 128.

30 General Services Administration Factsheet Concerning the Art-in-Architecture Program for Federal Buildings, in Martha Buskirk and Clara Weyergraf-Serra, eds., *The Destruction of Tilted Arc: Documents* (Cambridge: MIT Press, 1991), 23.

31 See Douglas Crimp, "Serra's Public Sculpture: Redefining Site Specificity," in *Richard Serra: Sculpture* (New York: Museum of Modern Art, 1986), 40–56; and Deutsch, *Evictions*, 257–270.

32 Deutsche, *Evictions*, 261.

33 "Political" site specificity is Deutsche's term, used to distinguish it from "academic" site specificity. Ibid., 261–262.

34 Richard Serra, "*Tilted Arc* Destroyed" (1989), reprinted in Richard Serra, *Writings Interviews* (Chicago: University of Chicago Press, 1994), 193–213.

35 See Rosalyn Deutsche's critique of the conflation between permanence and universal timelessness during the *Tilted Arc* hearings, in *Evictions*, 264. See also Douglas Crimp's interview comments in "Douglas Crimp on *Tilted Arc*," in Tom Finklepearl, ed., *Dialogues in Public Art* (Cambridge, Mass.: MIT Press, 2000), 71.

36 Serra, "*Tilted Arc* Destroyed," 202.

37 Ibid.

38 Ibid., 203.

39 On this point, see Hal Foster, "The Un/making of Sculpture," in Russell Ferguson, Anthony McCall, and Clara Weyergraf-Serra, eds., *Richard Serra: Sculpture 1985–1998* (Los Angeles and Göttingen, Germany: Museum of Contemporary Art and Steidl Verlag, 1998).

40 Buskirk and Weyergraf-Serra, eds., *The Destruction of Tilted Arc,* 12.

41 Richard Serra's apparent animosity toward architecture is well known and well documented. See his comments in, for instance, his interviews with critic Douglas Crimp and architect Peter Eisenman, both reprinted in Serra, *Writings Interviews.* But Serra's "working against" architecture is not a straightforward opposition. For the most provocative interpretations of Serra's relationship to architecture, see Foster, "The Un/making of Sculpture," and Yve-Alain Bois, "A Picturesque Stroll around *Clara-Clara,*" *October* 29 (Summer 1984).

42 Foster, "The Un/making of Sculpture," 17.

43 Ibid., 14.

44 Rosalind Krauss has written: "The specificity of the site is not the subject of the work, but—in its articulation of the movement of the viewer's body-in-destination—its medium." Krauss, "Richard Serra Sculpture," in *Richard Serra: Sculpture* (1986), 37.

45 See Buskirk and Weyergraf-Serra, eds., *The Destruction of Tilted Arc,* for the record of statements given at the hearings.

46 Representative Theodore Weiss, in Buskirk and Weyergraf-Serra, *The Destruction of Tilted Arc,* 115.

47 Joseph Liebman's testimony, for example, paints the plaza prior to the installation of *Tilted Arc* as an idyllic setting with children playing, mothers strolling with baby carriages, etc. See Buskirk and Weyergraf-Serra, eds., *The Destruction of Tilted Arc,* 113. Such memory is strongly contradicted by Douglas Crimp, a resident of the neighborhood. See his remarks concerning the somewhat dysfunctional state of the plaza prior to *Tilted Arc* in "Douglas Crimp on *Tilted Arc,*" 71–72.

48 Deutsche, *Evictions,* 259.

49 Some prominent cases include Pablo Picasso's sculpture at the Chicago Civic Center (1965), Alexander Calder's *La Grande Vitesse* in Grand Rapids, Michigan (1967), George Sugarman's *Baltimore Federal* (1975–1977), and Maya Lin's Vietnam Veterans' Memorial in Washington,

D.C. (1982). For more on other public art controversies, see Senie, *Contemporary Public Sculpture,* especially chapter six, and Doss, *Spirit Poles and Flying Pigs.*

50 Initial goals of the NEA's Art-in-Public-Places Program as stated in its guidelines and cited in Finklepearl, ed., *Dialogues in Public Art,* 43.

51 Of course, Andres Serrano's *Piss Christ* and Robert Mapplethorpe's homosexually explicit X-portfolio photographs drew as much, if not more, attention during these years. See Richard Bolton, ed., *Culture Wars: Documents from the Recent Controversies in the Arts* (New York: New Press, 1992).

52 Deutsche, *Evictions,* 267.

53 Representative Theodore Weiss, in Buskirk and Weyergraf-Serra, eds., *The Destruction of Tilted Arc,* 116.

54 As cited in Lacy, ed., *Mapping the Terrain,* 22–24.

55 Suzanne Lacy has remarked that even with the "maturation" of site-specific public art through the 1980s, in which greater attention was paid to the historical, ecological, and sociological aspects of a site, the works generally did not engage audiences in a manner markedly different from those in museums. Lacy, ed., *Mapping the Terrain,* 23.

56 Ibid., 27.

57 Finklepearl, ed., *Dialogues in Public Art,* 34–35.

58 According to Lacy, the theorization of "new genre public art" emerged from a lecture program sponsored by the California College of Arts and Crafts in 1989 entitled "City Sites: Artists and Urban Strategies." "A series of lectures was delivered at nontraditional sites in Oakland by ten artists whose work addressed a particular constituency on specific issues but also stood as a prototype for a wider range of human concerns." The term was officially coined for a three-day symposium organized by Lacy and others, "Mapping the Terrain: New Genre Public Art," at the San Francisco Museum of Modern Art in November 1991. Lacy, ed., *Mapping the Terrain,* 11.

59 Ibid., 24.

60 Ibid.

61 Ibid.

62 Others not necessarily aligned with new genre public art have also registered a sense of disappointment at Serra's work not being "radical" enough. See Finklepearl, ed., *Dialogues in Public Art,* 35. See also James Meyer's critique of *Tilted Arc*'s "negative" monumentality in "The Functional Site," *Documents* 7 (Fall 1994): 20–29.

63 The phrase is borrowed from Stuart Hall's critique of the cultural politics of Margaret Thatcher's England in "Popular-Democratic vs Authoritarian Populism: Two Ways of 'Taking Democracy Seriously,'" in *The Hard Road to Renewal: Thatcherism and the Crisis of the Left* (London: Verso, 1988), 123–149. Rosalyn Deutsch explains the concept succinctly as "the mobilization of democratic discourses to sanction, indeed to pioneer, shifts toward state totalitarianism." Deutsche, *Evictions,* 266.

64 This undertheorized alliance set the stage for the identity politics and political correctness debates of the early 1990s. In terms of public art, little room was left for bold, ambitious artistic statements that did not engage social issues or the "community."

65 This directive expanded in the early 1990s to include "educational activities which invite community involvement." See Lacy, ed., *Mapping the Terrain,* 24. For a sample case of the shift in attitude toward greater community participation in public art, see Tom Finklepearl's assessment of the 1999 community cultural plan of Portland, Maine, in his *Dialogues in Public Art,* 43–44.

66 Finklepearl, ed., *Dialogues in Public Art,* 81.

67 Ibid., 81–82. Art historian Erika Doss has pointed out that "throughout the 1980s, the NEA [and state arts agencies] avoided funding public art projects that were specifically commemorative or representational," preferring modern abstract art of artists such as Stephen Antonakos, Robert Irwin, Richard Fleischner, Tony Smith, Mark di Suvero, Mary Miss, Athena Tacha, and Richard Serra. She argues that the aesthetic vocabulary of abstraction, which is not shared by the general audience (who seem to prefer easily understandable symbolism), is one main source of the many public art controversies of the 1980s. It is important to note that the NEA corrected itself in the late 1980s, however, with the following addition to their guidelines: "The [NEA] must not, under any circumstances, impose a single aesthetic standard or attempt to direct artistic content." Doss claims that with such a revised vision, the NEA increased funding for representational art, such as public murals, in the 1990s. See Doss, *Spirit Poles and Flying Pigs,* 51, fn. 24.

68 Finklepearl, ed., *Dialogues in Public Art,* 82.

69 John Ahearn, quoted in Jane Kramer, *Whose Art Is It?* (Durham: Duke University Press, 1994), 39. For a detailed overview of Ahearn's practice from 1979 to 1991, see the exhibition catalogue *South Bronx Hall of Fame: Sculptures by John Ahearn and Rigoberto Torres* (Houston: Contemporary Arts Museum, 1991).

70 For an informative review of art dealing with the stereotypes and realities of life in the Bronx, see *Urban Mythologies: The Bronx Represented since the 1960s* (Bronx: Bronx Museum of the Arts, 1999), the catalogue of an exhibition curated by Lydia Yee and Betti-Sue Hertz.

71 Ahearn as quoted in Kramer, *Whose Art Is It?,* 38.

72 Ibid., 74–75.

73 Serra, "*Tilted Arc* Destroyed," 203.

74 Torres worked first as an assistant, then as partner of Ahearn through the 1980s. They have each credited the other with opening up their work and life. See Kramer, *Whose Art Is It?,* especially pp. 58–60 and 120–125 on the relationship between the two artists.

75 Fashion Moda was an alternative gallery space founded by Stefan Eins, an Austrian artist, in 1978, that operated for about ten years. The importance of this space in the burgeoning of the "alternative scene" in the early 1980s cannot be underestimated. According to Marshall Berman's chronicle of the Bronx, "For a decade or more, Fashion Moda brought downtown artists, musicians, and writers together with uptown graffiti painters, rappers, break dance crews, and curious people who came in from off the street. Eins was immensely resourceful at working various government bureaucracies and helping artists get space to mount innovative installations in schools and parks, in abandoned apartment buildings (there were so many), and on the streets." See Marshall Berman, "Views from the Burning Bridge," in *Urban Mythologies,* exh. cat., 76. Also see Betti-Sue Hertz's essay "Artistic Intervention in the Bronx" in the same exhibition catalogue, 18–27.

76 John Ahearn as quoted in Kramer, *Whose Art Is It?,* 111.

77 Ahearn as quoted in ibid., 60.

78 Arthur Symes and Claudette LaMelle made these charges without actually seeing the work. Their criticism was based on a few Polaroid snapshots taken at the foundry before the sculp-

tures were painted. Perhaps for this reason they misidentified Raymond as black rather than Puerto Rican.

79 Kramer, *Whose Art Is It?*, 38.

80 Thanks to Juliet Koss for helpful discussions on the history of empathy theory in aesthetic philosophy.

81 Angela Salgado, as quoted by Kramer, *Whose Art Is It?*, 109.

82 Ibid., 100–102.

83 Quoted in ibid., 103.

84 "John Ahearn on the Bronx Bronzes and Happier Tales," in Finklepearl, ed., *Dialogues in Public Art,* 91–92.

85 For instance, in Ahearn's case, the artist viewed the primary audience as residents of the neighborhood and the police officers of the 44th Precinct, who would be literally facing the sculptures at the traffic triangle. In contrast, the opponents of the sculptures conceived the audience as being comprised of strangers from the "outside world," mostly white people passing by their neighborhood in cars on their way to nearby Yankee Stadium.

86 Kardon, "Street Wise/Street Foolish," 8.

87 On this important issue, see George Yudice, "Producing the Cultural Economy: The Col*labor*ative Art of inSITE," in his *The Expediency of Culture* (Durham: Duke University Press, forthcoming).

88 A reversal because the traditional avant-garde did not seek to affirm the subject but to shock it loose from the comfort and familiarity of bourgeois complacency.

89 This is a crucial insight offered by Rosalyn Deutsche. See her chapter "Agoraphobia," in *Evictions,* 269–327.

4

1 Beginning in 1983, Sculpture Chicago presented outdoor sculpture exhibitions and symposia, first annually, then biennially. Since the 1995–1996 program "Re-Inventing the Garden City,"

under the direction of Joyce Fernandes, Sculpture Chicago has been inactive. A major portion of the "Culture in Action" archive is currently housed in the library of the Center for Curatorial Studies at Bard College; all other files pertaining to Sculpture Chicago's activities are housed at the office of Robert Wislow, its founder and chair, in Chicago.

2 To say that the exhibition was "on view" is not strictly correct, since most of the projects in "Culture in Action" were event-oriented and not object-based. The broad geographical dispersion of projects across different locales in the city, on top of the very immateriality of the projects, made viewing the entire program a complicated challenge for anyone interested, especially for out-of-town visitors. In fact, the exhibition coalesced as such through its exhibition catalogue and other publicity materials.

Sculpture Chicago tried to facilitate the viewing through a series of eleven five-hour guided bus tours on select dates in the summer months of 1993. These bus tours were the primary means of physical access to the exhibition as a whole. Moreover, because the process-oriented nature of the projects required much narrative support, or simply explanation, even for those quite conversant with contemporary art, the bus tours became a primary source of interpretive access as well. Thus, audience access to the meaning of the individual projects—their ambitions, their formal and/or organizational structures, and their (im)material manifestations—became completely dependent on the "supplementary" offerings of the tour guide, usually a staff member from Sculpture Chicago. That a program devoted to inventing a new relationship between art and its audience resorted to such a hermetic interface between the two raises questions as to the general confusion between community and audience in new genre public art.

3 "Sculpture Chicago History and Present Program," undated press release, n.p.

4 See *Culture in Action,* exh. cat. (Seattle: Bay Press, 1995), for more detailed information on each project. It should be underlined, however, that a few projects—Ericson and Ziegler's *Eminent Domain* and Robert Peters's *Naming Others: Manufacturing Yourself* in particular—were not realized to the degree that the catalogue claims. For example, when "Culture in Action" opened in May 1993, Ericson and Ziegler's paint charts existed only as mockups. Visitors to the exhibition saw displays of the prototype at Ogden Courts but did not see them distributed in local stores, as was originally intended. Based on preliminary communication with True Test Manufacturing Company, the artists and Sculpture Chicago announced at this time that the charts would be distributed at True Value Hardware stores nationwide by the fall of 1993. But this promise was never fulfilled. Almost all critics of the exhibition, however, have addressed *Eminent Domain* in terms of its representation in the exhibition catalogue and other promotional literature, emphasizing the general primacy of discursive production (publicity) in constituting the meaning of artistic practice.

5 The change in exhibition title signals a major shift in the conceptual basis of the show, from public art as static objects (in the tradition of monuments) to public art as process-oriented actions. This change was originally suggested by artist Daniel Martinez.

6 Held from May 10 to October 27, 1989, this was a standard juried exhibition. The ten participating artists were Vito Acconci, Richard Deacon, Richard Serra, Judith Shea, Josh Garber, Sheila Klein, Daniel Peterman, David Schafer, Thomas Skomski, and Rogelio Tijerina. There was a blatant division of artists and their work in terms of their status in the international art scene. For example, the first four artists were given prominent city locations (Pioneer Court, the plaza in front of the Equitable Building on North Michigan Avenue) whereas the remaining six less-established artists were given a secondary location (Cityfront Center near the NBC Tower). Also, the first four simply installed their works for presentation whereas the remaining six had to fulfill the "Art-in-Progress" component of the program: they were set up in tents on site to work on their sculptures so that their "creative working process" could be viewed by the passing "public." This hierarchization of artists was repeated in the promotional materials including the catalogue, where the first four received luxurious treatment, with several pages of images and text for each, while the latter six were given short, one-paragraph descriptions.

7 Interview with the author, May 14, 1996.

8 Jacob has said that the progamming of "Culture in Action" was most directly inspired by David Hammon's *House of the Future,* a community-based project that was part of the 1991 Spoleto Festival exhibition "Places with a Past," which Jacob also curated. For more on Hammon's project, see the exhibition catalogue *Places with a Past: New Site-Specific Art at Charleston's Spoleto Festival* (New York: Rizzoli, 1991). See also Tom Finklepearl's comments in *Dialogues in Public Art* (Cambridge: MIT Press, 2000), 41–42.

9 The most prominent art world figures who have spoken in enthusiastic support of "Culture in Action" include David Ross, former director of the San Francisco Museum of Modern Art, and Arthur Danto, art critic for the *Nation.* See also Michael Brenson, "Healing in Time," in *Culture in Action,* 16–49; Edward J. Sozanski, "A New Spin on What Art Can Be When It Goes Public," *Philadelphia Inquirer,* August 22, 1993; and Suzi Gablik, "Removing the Frame: An Interview with 'Culture in Action' Curator Mary Jane Jacob," *New Art Examiner* (January 1994): 14–18. Art historian Patricia Phillips wrote: "This radical project left few assumptions about public art, perception, distribution, and roles of artists—and curators—unchallenged. 'Culture in Action' raised significant questions and issues that have renergized a dialogue on public art." Similarly, Lucy Lippard wrote in praise of the show's exhibition catalogue: "In the thirty years that the role and efficacy of an outreaching public art has been debated within the 'avant-

garde,' few books have stated the issues as clearly as *Culture in Action.* Mary Jane Jacob asks all the right questions, suggests some answers, and provides a new model in her curatorial practice." (Both references are from promotional material distributed by Brunsman & Associates on behalf of Sculpture Chicago.)

10 See, for example, Michael Kimmelman's review of the exhibition, "Of Candy Bars and Public Art," *New York Times,* September 26, 1993, 2:1, 43; Eleanor Heartney, "The Dematerialization of Public Art," *Sculpture* (March-April 1993): 45–49, "'Culture in Action' at Various Sites," *Art in America* (November 1993); Joseph Scanlon, "Joseph Scanlon on Sculpture Chicago's Culture in Action," *Frieze* (November-December 1993): 22–27; and Hafthor Yngvason, "The New Public Art: As Opposed to What?" *Public Art Review* (Spring/Summer 1993): 4–5.

11 The exhibition included temporary projects by Joseph Bartscherer, Gloria Bornstein and Donald Fels, Cris Bruch, Chris Burden, General Idea, Group Material, Edgar Heap of Birds, Robert Herdlein, Gary Hill, Ilya Kabakov, Alan Lande, David Mahler, Daniel Martinez, Martha Rosler, Norie Sato, and Lewis "Buster" Simpson. The two permanent projects were Jonathan Borofsky's sculpture *Hammering Man* in front of the new Seattle Art Museum (a building designed by the office of Robert Venturi and Denise Scott Brown) and a collaborative installation at Pier 62/63 by Laurie Hawkinson (architect), Barbara Kruger (artist), Guy Nordenson (structural engineer), Nicholas Quennell (landscape architect), Henry Smith-Miller (architect), and Gail Dubrow (Seattle historian). For more detailed information on this exhibition, see *In Public: Seattle 1991,* exh. cat. (Seattle: Seattle Arts Commission, 1992).

12 See Richard Andrews, "Artists and the Visual Definition of Cities: The Experience of Seattle," in Stacy Paleologos Harris, ed., *Insights/On Sites: Perspectives on Art in Public Places* (Washington, D.C.: Partners for Livable Places, 1984), 16–23. See also Richard Andrews, Jim Hirschfield, and Larry Rausch, *Artwork/Network: A Planning Study for Seattle, Art in the Civic Context* (Seattle: Seattle Arts Commission, 1988).

13 See chapter 3 on the complications of the design team model.

14 T. Ellen Sollod, executive director of the Seattle Art Commission, in *In Public: Seattle 1991,* 7.

15 The rhetoric around the innovation of "Culture in Action" continues to highlight the community-based collaborative element. Mary Jane Jacob herself embraced it as a distinctive aspect of the exhibition: "[Culture in Action] is the result of a fundamental collaboration among participating artists, community residents, and civic leaders. This collaborative process has to an unusual degree shaped the conception as well as the realization of these artists' projects, and led to a new dialogue between the artist and audience for public art." (Quoted in "Urban

Issues Are Focus of New Public Art Program in Chicago," undated press release, 1–2.) But there was greater institutional and curatorial ambivalence, if not resistance, to the community-based collaborations than is acknowledged. According to my research, Jacob and Sculpture Chicago were reluctant to foreground the community when naming the projects during the early phase of the exhibition's development. Artists Kate Ericson and Mel Ziegler in fact disputed with them over the ways in which the role of the community was diminished in relation to the artists in Sculpture Chicago's public announcements regarding "Culture in Action." Ericson and Ziegler successfully insisted on equal billing (in the treatment of the community name in all published materials) and unsuccessfully sought monetary compensation for the community in letters dated between late November 1992 and early February 1993.

Jacob remembers this dispute differently (as not a dispute at all). For example, in her interview with Annette DiMeo Carlozzi in *Art Papers* 21, no. 3 (May/June 1997): 8–13, she states that "we realized halfway through the process that all the artists were working collaboratively, actually determining their pieces with members of the public. I just suggested that maybe all these projects should change their names to include the community."

16 Picasso's *The Head of a Woman,* the artist's first large-scale urban sculpture, was funded by private money ($300,000) and resulted from architect William Hartmann's (of Skidmore, Owings and Merrill) desire to model the Chicago Civic Center on the European piazza. The project set an influential precedent for artists and architects involved in public art commissions for the next decade or more. For specific details on the Picasso commission, see Harriet F. Senie, *Contemporary Public Sculpture: Tradition, Transformation, and Controversy* (New York: Oxford University Press, 1992), 95–100.

17 Sponsored by Sculpture Chicago, Pritzker Park was a conscious departure from the organization's regular summer sculpture exhibitions described earlier.

18 The temporal framework for the exhibition, however, was strictly limited in legal terms. Once the artists' proposals were approved in summer 1992, contracts were distributed by Sculpture Chicago. The legal agreement, covering October 1, 1992 to September 30, 1993, bound the artists not only to complete their projects for presentation for "public viewing" from May 1 to September 30, 1993, but to perform particular publicity and promotional duties preceding and during this period. It should be noted that there were no such legal agreements between Sculpture Chicago and members of any of the participating community groups.

Ericson and Ziegler vehemently challenged Sculpture Chicago's withdrawal of financial and institutional support following the closing of "Culture in Action," raising the question: When is a project really over? The artists believed that Sculpture Chicago was financially and morally responsible for the "completion" of *Eminent Domain,* which included the nationwide distribution of the paint charts. Sculpture Chicago felt that its obligation to the artists and their project was met within the context of "Culture in Action," and that if the artists were interested in pursuing it further they should find another source of support. Even though True Test agreed to "host" the project in spring 1994 (over six months after the exhibition's closing), Sculpture Chicago felt that, without a promotional tie-in to a major cultural event, the meaning of the project would be completely lost to the random paint customer, resulting in a waste of time and money for all involved. The artists accused Sculpture Chicago of using them and the community resident group for its own public relations purposes, and charged that the overall conceptual frame of "Culture in Action" was hypocritical. Sculpture Chicago in turn viewed the artists as inflexible and impractical.

To ameliorate the situation, Sculpture Chicago considered a "kill fee" for the project (though this did not materialize) and, at the insistence of the artists, paid the resident group $3,000 for their involvement in "Culture in Action." But the situation was further exacerbated when Ericson and Ziegler refused to contribute any materials to the exhibition catalogue, which they deemed another form of Sculpture Chicago's self-promotion. This refusal led Sculpture Chicago to solicit the assistance of Kelly Rogers of the Sidley Austin law office to clarify that the artists had a legal obligation to provide materials for the catalogue. In the end, it seems no one wanted to pursue a legal battle, and the artists reluctantly contributed their work to the catalogue, quibbling over the wording of certain aspects of the project description as authored by Mary Jane Jacob.

19 See chapter 3, note 58, on the discursive genesis of new genre public art.

20 Suzanne Lacy, "Cultural Pilgrimages and Metaphoric Journeys," in Lacy, ed., *Mapping the Terrain,* 19.

21 Ibid., 20.

22 Arlene Raven, ed., *Art in the Public Interest* (1989; New York: Da Capo Press, 1993).

23 Ibid., 1.

24 Ibid., 4.

25 Ibid., 18.

26 Lacy, "Cultural Pilgrimages," 25.

27 Ibid., 20.

28 See Jeff Kelley, "Common Work," in Lacy, ed., *Mapping the Terrain,* 139–148. Tom Finklepearl has similarly opposed the "art of abstraction" (modernism) to the "art of attraction" (participatory modes of public art practice). See his essay "Abstraction and Attraction," in *Uncommon Sense,* exh. cat. (Los Angeles: Museum of Contemporary Art, Los Angeles, 1997), 13–34.

29 For a countertheorization of the concept of democracy in relation to public art, see Rosalyn Deutsche, *Evictions: Art and Spatial Politics* (Cambridge: MIT Press, 1996), especially the chapter "Agoraphobia."

30 Mary Jane Jacob, as quoted in Lacy, ed., *Mapping the Terrain,* 30. What does it mean for a particular mode of practice to "find its time"? This is a historiographical question. Just as certain historical, political, social, economic, and aesthetic conditions influence the emergence of new modes of cultural practice, signaling tendencies both large and small, the broadening acceptance of an old mode of cultural practice (sometimes in the form of a return) similarly points to the conjuncture of such influences.

31 Heartney, "The Dematerialization of Public Art," 45.

32 Jeff Kelley, as quoted in Lacy, "Cultural Pilgrimages," 24. Such a statement does not acknowledge the extent to which certain site-specific art has critically questioned the "museum zone" itself. It also presupposes the museum as a closed system, the status of which has also been challenged via site-specific practices over the past three decades. See chapter 1.

33 For an extensive history of the philosophical distinctions between space, place, and site, see Edward Casey, *The Fate of Place: A Philosophical History* (Berkeley: University of California Press, 1997).

34 Kelley, "Common Work," 141. A similar sensibility rules Lucy Lippard's *The Lure of the Local: A Sense of Place in a Multicultural Society* (New York: New Press, 1997), which also emphasizes place as holistic culture (as opposed to the abstraction of "site"). See chapter 6 for a critique of Lippard's position.

35 Interview with the author, November 7, 1995.

36 Mary Jane Jacob, "Urban Issues Are Focus of New Public Art Program in Chicago," undated press release, 2.

37 Mary Jane Jacob as quoted in "Sculpture Chicago Receives Major Funding Support for Public Art Initiative," press release, March 10, 1993, n.p.

38 Dan Cameron, "'Culture in Action': Eliminate the Middleman," *Flash Art* (November/December 1993): 62.

39 Heartney, "The Dematerialization of Public Art," 45.

40 Mary Jane Jacob, "Outside the Loop," in *Culture in Action,* 56.

41 The call for the rehabilitation of public art happens to coincide with revisions in operational guidelines of major private and public funding sources for art in general and public art in particular. For example, in the mid 1990s, the MacArthur Foundation redirected its support of media arts to "community-based organizations that are working to promote social justice and democracy through the media"; the Lila Wallace/Reader's Digest Foundation limited its artist funding to those who work explicitly with "communities"; and, more drastically, the Lannan Foundation in Los Angeles shifted from arts funding to projects in support of "social issues," giving up collecting art altogether.

42 Heather Mac Donald, "The New Community Activism: Social Justice Comes Full Circle," *City Journal* (August 1993): 44–55. Thanks to Rosalyn Deutsche for directing my attention to this reference.

43 Ibid., 44.

44 Ibid., 48.

45 Ibid., 46.

46 Ibid., 53. Throughout the text, the author (perhaps rightly) characterizes existing social services as ineffectual and inefficient. But the author also makes the rather outrageous claim that those working in the social services "industry" purposefully *cultivate* poverty, illness, and other social ills in order to further increase their business and to expand their authoritative power.

47 In what has by now become a familiar mode of operation, Jacob and Sculpture Chicago organized a symposium that took place on December 5, 1992, approximately six months *prior* to the general public opening of the exhibition. Over seventy-five guests were invited, including museum professionals from across the United States, curators from Europe, art critics and journalists, architects, university professors, public arts administrators, local community leaders, public relations experts, delegates from funding organizations, representatives of community groups engaged in "Culture in Action" projects, and, of course, the artists and the

Sculpture Chicago staff. One part of the symposium addressed questions such as: "How can artists work with communities that are not their own? How can public art contribute to a community? Can art empower a community? What particular obstacles or problems face the artists participating in Sculpture Chicago's 'Culture in Action'? What are these artists attempting to accomplish?" The second part addressed more general issues concerning the relevance of this new public art in relation to the organization of the urban environment, audience/constituency, art history, other art institutions, art education, etc.

Although some of the "Culture in Action" artists who were able to participate presented their work in progress for feedback, it is difficult to gauge whether, and to what extent, the symposium had any direct bearing on the outcome of their projects. Most had already passed the proposal stage, and the implementation of the projects was well under way by the time of the symposium. It is certain, however, that the gathering of so many arts-related professionals had a big impact on the *reception* of "Culture in Action" insofar as the symposium not only put the word out early but preemptively posed critical questions that the artists and the organization would have to face later on.

In conversations with the author, several artists from "Culture in Action" registered their suspicion of the motivations behind the symposium. Rather than an attempt to generate broad theoretical discussions on the state of public art, they believed it served primarily to promote and publicize the exhibition, within which the artist had little choice but to participate as a kind of spokesperson for the exhibition.

48 Yngvason, "The New Public Art," 5.

49 Ibid. The internal quotations reference Seyla Benhabib, *Situating the Self: Gender, Community and Postmodernism in Contemporary Ethics* (New York: Routledge, 1992), 79.

50 The projects in "Culture in Action" have been judged either by a standard deferral to aesthetic quality (measured against existing categories of sculpture, performance, video, installation, etc.) or in relation to a vague sense of political efficacy and public/audience engagement. For most critics, success in the former realm rarely translates to success in the latter. The criteria of social relevance and aesthetic quality seem to maintain an inversely proportional relation.

51 Lacy as quoted in Jacob, *Culture in Action*, 70.

52 Ibid., 69.

53 Iris Marion Young, "The Ideal of Community and the Politics of Difference," in Linda J. Nicholson, ed., *Feminism/Postmodernism* (New York: Routledge, 1990), 301.

54 In large-scale performance projects throughout the 1970s and 1980s, Lacy tended toward similarly essentialized representations of women as a social category, bound together primarily by a sense of injustice in the face of the patriarchal social order. Her well-known projects include *Inevitable Association* (1976), *In Mourning and in Rage* (1977), *Whisper, the Waves, the Wind* (1984), *Crystal Quilt* (1987), and *Underground* (1993). For an overview of Lacy's practice, see Jeff Kelley, "The Body Politics of Suzanne Lacy," in Nina Felshin, ed., *But Is It Art? The Spirit of Art as Activism* (Seattle: Bay Press, 1995), 221–249.

55 I am borrowing this phrase from Hal Foster as it appears in his essay, "The Artist as Ethnographer," in *The Return of the Real: The Avant-Garde at the End of the Century* (Cambridge: MIT Press, 1996), 171–203.

56 Technically, Grennan and Sperandio were not complete outsiders in that they had both studied in the graduate art program at the University of Illinois, Chicago; they had recently graduated when first approached by Mary Jane Jacob. According to Sperandio, their inclusion in "Culture in Action" probably resulted from the fact that they were, at the time of the exhibition's preliminary planning, Chicago-based. This fact would have counted toward Jacob's need to include local artists in her program.

57 Under such circumstances, in which an artist from out of town has to convince a nonart organization to spend time and effort, and sometimes money, to engage in a public art project, the artist's (and perhaps more importantly the curator's) charisma, his/her power of persuasion, his/her ability to establish a rapport with and to gain trust from potential participants, becomes crucial to the success of the project.

58 Simon Grennan and Christopher Sperandio, undated project proposal. Of all the artists in "Culture in Action," Grennan and Sperandio most explicitly adopt the language—both discursive and visual—of corporate culture for the presentation of their proposals. Their practice serves as an interesting example of the "administration of aesthetics" mode of practice as described in chapter 2.

59 Kate Ericson and Mel Ziegler, letter to Mary Jane Jacob and Eva Olson, dated June 14, 1992. The idea of producing a color paint chart that would deal with the history of federally sponsored housing in the United States as a public art project can be traced to Ericson and Ziegler's site-specific work in Charleston, South Carolina, in the summer of 1991. There, in the context of their research for the city-based exhibition "Places with a Past: New Site-Specific Art at Charleston's Spoleto Festival," also curated by Jacob, the artists discovered a paint chart produced by Dutch Boy entitled "The Authentic Colors of Historic Charleston." This paint chart, developed specifically with historic preservation in mind, presented not only

various color choices available for restoring the "Charleston look" of a local building, but also a timeline of U.S. and Charleston history (from 1660 to 1900) accompanied by a chart of changing architectural styles of the region through the same period. This chart served as a template for Ericson and Ziegler in their conception of a possible public art project for Chicago. For more details on their Charleston project (entitled *Camouflaged History*), see the exhibition catalogue *Places with a Past,* 176–181.

60 Mary Jane Jacob as quoted in "Urban Issues Are Focus of New Public Art Program in Chicago," undated press release, 1–2. The "other exhibitions of site-specific installation art-works" that Jacob is referring to here are international in scope and include "Places with a Past: New Site-Specific Art at Charleston's Spoleto Festival," curated by Jacob in Charleston, South Carolina, May 24–August 4, 1991; "Project Unité," curated by Yves Apetitallot in Firminy, France, June 1–September 30, 1993; "Sonsbeek '93," curated by Valerie Smith in Arnhem, Netherlands, June 5–September 26, 1993; and "On Taking a Normal Situation and Retranslating It into Overlapping and Multiple Readings of Conditions Past and Present," curated by Iwona Blazwick, Yves Apetitallot, and Carolyn Christov-Bakargiev as part of the Antwerp '93 celebration in Antwerp, Belgium, September 18–November 28, 1993.

61 Joyce Fernandes, who took over leadership of Sculpture Chicago as its program director after the conclusion of "Culture in Action" and the departure of Jacob, specifically tried to address this problem in the next Sculpture Chicago program, "Re-inventing the Garden City" (1995–1996). By pairing artists with community groups earlier in the process, Fernandes hoped to engage community participation in the *conceptualization* of an art project at the proposal stage. Because all the projects were determined to address specified public parks as sites of social activity, potential collaborators were easily found around Washington Square Park/Bughouse Square, Union Park, Garfield Park, and Humboldt Park. The community groups were to "reinvent" a more clear-cut sense of identity and proprietorship over the park's territory and activities. But this made the collaborative process more difficult in some cases, as the artist was pushed to the margins of the conceptualization process. Dennis Adams, one of four artists involved in the "Re-inventing" program, dropped out of the project due to unresolvable disagreements with community leaders at Garfield Park. The key issue in such community-based collaborations seems to be the difficulty of striking the right balance among the participants—i.e., the sharing of authority. Miroslaw Rogala, Ellen Rothenberg, and Pepón Osorio were the other participating artists, and their projects at the three other parks were on view from June 8 to September 7, 1996.

62 See, for instance, the comments of Eleanor Heartney in "The Dematerialization of Public Art," 45–49; and Allison Gamble, "Reframing a Movement: Sculpture Chicago's 'Culture in Action,'" *New Art Examiner* (January 1994): 18–23.

63 See Mary Jane Jacob's interview with Annette DiMeo Carlozzi, "Questioning the Questioner," *Art Papers* 21, no. 3 (May/June 1997): 8–13.

64 See the comments of Ukeles in her conversation with Doug Ashford, "Democracy Is Empty," *Documents* 10 (Fall 1997): 23–30. According to Ukeles, these types of "curatorial assignments" are usually conceived in reductive terms, as "self-esteem workshops" or "community fix-up" projects.

65 Christopher Sperandio in conversation with the author, November 7, 1995.

66 Letter from Mary Jane Jacob to Elaine Reichek dated September 1992. My description of Reichek's proposal in the preceding paragraph is derived from the artist's communication (semiofficial, including a preliminary budget for the project) to Mary Jane Jacob dated August 7, 1992. In addition to Reichek, other artists approached for "Culture in Action" in the early stages of its planning include Mary Ellen Carroll, Mel Chin, Alfredo Jaar, and Renée Green. These artists were not included in the exhibition for reasons ranging from scheduling problems to practicalities of the proposals to ideological differences. On Green's exchange with Sculpture Chicago, see chapter 5.

67 Mark Dion, undated and unpublished statement prepared for a public presentation on his project in early 1993. The statement is particularly interesting for the ways that the "site" is conceived as available social relations. The overall framing of Dion's statement is to clarify his notion of an "integrated [art] practice."

68 Gamble, "Reframing a Movement," 22.

69 Manglano-Ovalle removed himself from the position of director of Street-Level Video soon after the conclusion of "Culture in Action," leaving the responsibility of sustaining the project to the younger participants, who came to view themselves as artists in their own right. The current mission statement of Street-Level Youth Media found on its website expands on many of the original objectives: "Street-Level Youth Media educates Chicago's inner-city youth in media arts and emerging technologies for use in self-expression, communication and social change. Street-Level's programs build self-esteem and critical thinking skills for urban youth who have been historically neglected by policy makers and mass media. Using video production, computer art and the Internet, Street-Level's young people address community issues, access advanced communication technology and gain inclusion in our information-based society." According to the website, over 1,200 youths in neighborhoods across Chicago participated in its programs in 2000. Interestingly, there is no mention of "Culture in Action" in the narrative regarding the program's history. The 1993 street video installation and block

party are described as "the first summer" of the project. For more information on current activities and programs of Street-Level Youth Media, see http://streetlevel.iit.edu.

70 Sometimes these efforts are too prescriptive. See artist Renée Green's comments regarding her exchanges with Mary Jane Jacob and Sculpture Chicago in the chapter 5.

71 This shift in function was well understood by Manglano-Ovalle, whose block party resituated Sculpture Chicago from institutional host of the event to neighborhood guest.

5

1 Hal Foster, "The Artist as Ethnographer," in his *The Return of the Real: The Avant-Garde at the End of the Century* (Cambridge: MIT Press, 1996).

2 Ibid., 196. Foster's example is Clegg & Guttmann's project for the exhibition "Project Unité" in Firminy, France, curated by Yves Apetitallot (June 1–September 30, 1993). For the show, a group of artists were commissioned to create site-specific installations inside the residential units at the Unité d'Habitation in Firminy, a building designed in the late 1950s by Le Corbusier as a model of modern urban living that is now occupied primarily by immigrant working-class families.

3 Ibid., 197. The passage is emphasized in the original.

4 Ibid., 190. Foster is referencing Bourdieu's *Outline of a Theory of Practice,* trans. Richard Nice (Cambridge: Cambridge University Press, 1977).

5 Foster describes the phenomenon this way: "The local and the everyday are thought to resist economic development, yet they can also attract it, for such development needs the local and the everyday even as it erodes these qualities, renders them siteless. . . . Killed as culture, the local and the everyday can be revived as simulacrum, a 'theme' for a park or a 'history' in a mall, and site-specific work can be drawn into this zombification of the local and the everyday, this Disney version of the site-specific." Foster, *The Return of the Real,* 197.

6 Ibid., 196–197.

7 Grant Kester, "Aesthetic Evangelists: Conversion and Empowerment in Contemporary Community Art," *Afterimage* (January 1995): 5–11.

8 Pierre Bourdieu, "Delegation and Political Fetishism," in John B. Thompson, ed., *Language and*

Symbolic Power (Cambridge: Harvard University Press, 1994).

9 Kester, "Aesthetic Evangelists," 6. He cites in particular artist Hope Sandrow's comment on her relationship to the Artist and Homeless Collaborative, which she founded. For more on Sandrow, see Andrea Wolper, "Making Art, Reclaiming Lives: The Artist and Homeless Collaborative," in Nina Felshin, ed., *But Is It Art? The Spirit of Art as Activism* (Seattle: Bay Press, 1995), 251–282.

10 Kester, "Aesthetic Evangelists," 6.

11 Ibid. Bourdieu describes this process as an "embezzlement."

12 Renée Green was somewhat confounded by the ways in which she and her work were described in the biographical statement and project description authored by Sculpture Chicago, which she saw for the first time during an interview with the author on April 28, 1997.

13 Such reconnaissance trips are standard for artists engaged in these kinds of on-site, temporary-project-oriented, often community-based practices. See chapter 2, section on "Itinerant Artists."

14 According to the tentative travel itinerary found in the Sculpture Chicago files in 1996, Green's trip included a visit to the DuSable Museum of African-American Art; Providence-St. Mel High School, located in an African American neighborhood near Garfield Park that is troubled by unemployment and high crime rates; and meetings with Jim Grossman, the author of *Land of Hope: Chicago, Black Southerners and the Great Migration,* Charles Branham, professor of history at Northwestern University, and Amina Dickerson, director of education and public programs at the Chicago Historical Society.

15 Actually, how the relationship ended is ambiguous. Green does not recall being officially disinvited; Sculpture Chicago may never have felt the need to disinvite her since she had never been officially invited to participate in the first place (no contracts were signed at the point of the initial visit). Yet each party seems to have understood the other's agenda well enough after Green's visit to Chicago to refrain from further communication.

16 See this and other relevant comments by Green in the roundtable discussion "On Site Specificity," *Documents* 4–5 (Spring 1994): 11–22.

17 Hal Foster has described the problematic effects of such anticipation and projection as fol-

lows: "Often artist and community are linked through an identitarian reduction of both, the apparent authenticity of the one invoked to guarantee that of the other, in a way that threatens to collapse new site-specific work into identity politics *tout court.* As the artist stands *in* the identity of a sited community, he or she may be asked to stand *for* this identity, to represent it institutionally. In this case the artist is primitivized, indeed anthropologized, in turn: here is your community, the institution says in effect, embodied in your artist, now on display." Foster, *The Return of the Real,* 198.

18 Early in his essay, Kester does mention the extent to which community-based artists today collaborate with a more complex network of "professional institutions and ideologies that the artist . . . , in some cases, seeks to radicalize or challenge." (Kester, "Aesthetic Evangelists," 5.) But the role of these institutions and ideologies in determining the nature of the collaborations themselves seems to drop out in his subsequent discussion. This is one of the few shortcomings of Kester's text: he describes the relationship between artist and community group as immediate and direct, which is usually not the case.

19 Ibid., 7. According to Kester, the conservative arguments that define the current political climate in the United States have "successfully repudiated the 'excesses' of state intervention during the New Deal and the Great Society, portraying any attempt by the government to intervene into the 'natural' play of market forces as precipitating a moral crisis in capitalist culture in which the poor will refuse to work and will make unreasonable claims for unearned 'entitlements.'" He goes on to say:

> The cause of poverty in this scenario is not the systematic structure of capitalist labor markets and investment decisions within the context of the global economy but, rather, the moral inferiority of the individual subject (which is in turn the partial product of a polluted culture). . . . Conservatives argue that the real problem in the U.S. today is a lack of moral character among individuals, and that existing social problems can best be solved not by the state, but by the efforts of private individuals and organizations that develop programs focused on building the character of the poor. Thus we have moral pedagogy (designed to counter the "bad" moral pedagogy of the state) rather than any real attempt to alleviate the actual conditions of poverty and joblessness, much less any attempt to address their root causes.

20 This evangelical sensibility was explicit in curator Mary Jane Jacob's legitimating description of the premise of "Culture in Action": "In the 1990s the role of public art has shifted from that of renewing the physical environment to that of improving society, from promoting aesthetic quality to contributing to the quality of life, from enriching lives to saving lives." See her essay

"Outside the Loop," in *Culture in Action,* exh. cat. (Seattle: Bay Press, 1995).

21 From the Artist and Homeless Collaborative statement of purpose as cited by Kester. Kester cites another statement, by a member of John Malpede's performance group Los Angeles Poverty Department (LAPD), to exemplify the extent to which community-based art valorizes individual transformation in preference to analysis of social conditions: "I was a drunken sot living under a bush in Santa Monica, stealing beer. Now I live in a great apartment and I just directed a show. It was a great experience. I never thought I ever had a chance to do anything in the art world and I had very low self-esteem about being successful in any way. Now, after five years of being an actor in LAPD I feel really confident." Kester, "Aesthetic Evangelists," 8.

22 Martha Fleming, letter to the editor, *Afterimage* (June 1995): 3. While almost all artists involved in community-based art would deny (as Fleming does in her letter) that they ever speak for a community or have a privileged relationship to it, very few can articulate their position or process with as much critical self-reflection and fullness of feeling as Fleming. In this sense Fleming is one of the exceptional voices in the field.

23 Ibid.

24 Ibid.

25 Kester, "Aesthetic Evangelists," 6.

26 See chapters 1 and 2.

27 Kester, "Aesthetic Evangelists," 6.

28 Ibid.

29 One such example is the Three Rivers Arts Festival in Pittsburgh. In the summer of 1996, the organizers of this annual event, originally designed to draw people to the city's downtown, initiated a community-based public art program called "Points of Entry" following the model of "Culture in Action." Mary Jane Jacob was called in as a consultant on the project but withdrew halfway through the process. In an interview with the author (March 12, 1996), Jacob remarked of "Points of Entry": "All of [the] projects can be summarized as (A) artist, (B) group, on (C) issues. And that's neat. But I almost see a parody of myself here. It's so much 'Culture in Action' turned into a formula and not problematizing it." See also my review of "Points of Entry," "Three Rivers Arts Festival: Pittsburgh, PA," *Documents* 7(Fall 1996): 30–32.

30 Kester, "Aesthetic Evangelists," 6.

31 This was precisely the premise of Group Material's contribution to the 1996 "Points of Entry" exhibition at the Three Rivers Arts Festival in Pittsburgh. They used the exhibition guide as the site of intervention, incorporating divergent and contradictory comments from residents (gathered through extensive interviews), local businessmen, city officials, academics, urban theorists, and cultural critics into the official language of the publicity material. The project intended a disarticulation of the notion of community as put upon the artists by the organizers of the exhibition. See "Points of Entry," program guide (Pittsburgh: Three Rivers Arts Festival, 1996).

32 Kester writes, "This [politically-coherent community] formation almost always takes place against the grain of the dominant culture, which survives by individualizing social relationships in which the distribution of power is based on differences of class, race, gender, and sexuality. . . .The politically-coherent community can come into existence almost anywhere there are individuals who have struggled to identify their common interests (and common enemies) over and against a social system that is dedicated to denying the existence of systematic forms of oppression." Kester, "Aesthetic Evangelists," 6.

33 See my comments in chapter 4 on Heather Mac Donald's article "The New Community Activism: Social Justice Comes Full Circle," *City Journal* (Autumn 1993): 44–55. Adopting a victim discourse, those with cultural, financial, and political capital frequently characterize their positions of privilege as marginal now, especially in relation to the supposed authoritarian intervention of the (liberal) state overrun by politically correct dogmatism (it is argued that one can be unfairly marginalized *because* of privilege). A similar logic structures neoconservative arguments for "new citizenship" and "new civil society." See, for example, William A. Schambra, "By the People: The Old Values of the New Citizenship," *Policy Review* (Summer 1994): 32–39.

34 Kester, "Aesthetic Evangelists," 5–6. He suggests such an approach specifically as an alternative to the tendency toward the fetishization of authenticity, on the one hand, and a kind of poststructuralist "denuding," on the other, "which views the artist's transgressions of (what are seen as wholly arbitrary) social and cultural identities as inherently liberatory." According to Kester, these are two typical reactions in the art world to the fact that the exchange between a community group and an artist is never entirely organic.

35 Fleming, letter to the editor, 3.

36 Chantal Mouffe, "Citizenship and Political Identity," *October* 61 (Summer 1992): 28.

37 Here I am piggybacking on Bruce Robbins's characterization of the public sphere as a phantom in his introduction to Robbins, ed., *The Phantom Public Sphere* (Minneapolis: University of Minnesota Press, 1993), vii–xxvi. The benefits of such a concept have been outlined by Rosalyn Deutsche in her essay "Agoraphobia" in *Evictions: Art and Spatial Politics* (Cambridge: MIT Press, 1996), 320–321. My reading of the discourse on community is indebted especially to Deutsche's work.

38 See Iris Marion Young, "The Ideal of Community and the Politics of Difference," in Linda J. Nicholson, ed., *Feminism/ Postmodernism* (New York: Routledge, 1990), 300–323.

39 Ibid., 300.

40 Georges Van Den Abbeele describes two different types of communities based on two possible etymological roots of the word: first, from "*com* + *munis* (that is, with the sense of being bound, obligated, or indebted together)," and second, from "the more folk-etymological combination of *com* + *unus* (or what is together as one.)" The former, which describes a notion of community bound by a sense of mutual indebtedness, corresponds to the idea of community as a kind of social contract ("popularized by Locke and the Enlightenment *philosophes*"); the latter describes a notion of community as an organicist "body politic" ("colloquially linked to the name of Hobbes"). See Van Den Abbeele's introduction to Miami Theory Collective, ed., *Community at Loose Ends* (Minneapolis: University of Minnesota Press, 1991), xi. Young's notion of an ideal community coincides with Van Den Abbeele's second description: community as the absorption of singularities into oneness.

41 Young, "The Ideal of Community and the Politics of Difference," 302.

42 Ibid.

43 Ibid., 320.

44 Ibid., 302.

45 Rosalyn Deutsche comments on the effect of this seeming reversal in Young's thesis: "Young's politics of difference glosses over [important questions facing the politics of pluralism], defining difference as the 'particularity of entities,' although she says that particularity is socially constructed. As a result, Young does not consider the productive role that can be played by disruption, rather than consolidation, in the construction of identity, a disruption in which groups encounter their own uncertainty." (Deutsche, *Evictions*, 322; see pp. 309–310, 321–322 for a more extensive response to Young's thesis.) Deutsche's concern is primarily with the

constitution of the public sphere and not with the community per se.

46 Critical Art Ensemble, *Electronic Civil Disobedience and Other Unpopular Ideas* (Brooklyn, N.Y.: Autonomedia, 1996), 43–44.

47 Ibid., 45.

48 The mode of practice favored by CAE is nomadic and tactical, outside institutionally sanctioned forms, spaces, and contexts. Very much informed by situationist strategies, they have abandoned the belief in the realistic possibility of a mass social revolution but continue to believe in the power of small "subversive" acts that can provide momentary disruptions in the everyday maintenance of the rationalized order of society. The language of their avant-gardism tends to be strident if not militaristic.

49 The Rockefeller Foundation's Project Against Community Tension (PACT) is an example of this trend. See Iñigo Manglano-Ovalle, "Who Made Us the Target of Your Outreach?," *High Performance* (Winter 1994): 15–16.

50 Jean-Luc Nancy, "Of Being-in-Common," in Miami Theory Collective, ed., *Community at Loose Ends,* 4.

51 Ibid.

52 Van Den Abbeele, introduction to *Community at Loose Ends,* xiv. *La communauté désoeuvrée* is the original French title of Jean-Luc Nancy's collection of essays on the community (Paris: Christian Bourgois Editeur, 1986). The three essays in the French edition plus two additional essays comprise the English edition of Nancy's work, in which the word *désoeuvrée* is translated as "inoperative." See Jean-Luc Nancy, *The Inoperative Community* (Minneapolis: University of Minnesota Press, 1991).

53 In some respects, the one remaining project from "Culture in Action," which I have not discussed thus far, marks an impossibility of community, but only by default and only in a highly unproductive manner. In adopting a polling model of social interaction and communication, Robert Peters's phone survey project further individualizes such processes and reduces the possible discourses on community and difference to "yes" and "no" options. See *Culture in Action,* exh. cat. (Seattle: Bay Press, 1995), for a detailed description of the project.

54 I am extrapolating from cultural theorist Linda Singer's proposal that we can think of the community not as a referential sign but as a call or appeal to a collective praxis. Linda Singer, as

paraphrased by Georges Van Den Abbeele in his introduction to Miami Theory Collective, ed., *Community at Loose Ends,* xiv.

55 The "modeling" or "patterning" of a social relation should not be confused with the idea of a "model" or "pattern" of a social relation. The latter implies the establishment of a social template of sorts that can be copied and repeated. In specifically proposing a transitive action, I mean to emphasize the simultaneous process of coming together and coming apart of social relations. Thanks to Doug Ashford for discussions concerning the distinction between the descriptive and projective modes of community-based art practice.

6

1 Kenneth Frampton, "Towards a Critical Regionalism: Six Points for an Architecture of Resistance," in Hal Foster, ed., *The Anti-Aesthetic* (Port Townsend, Wash.: Bay Press, 1983), 26.

2 David Harvey, "From Space to Place and Back Again: Reflections on the Condition of Postmodernity," text for UCLA GSAUP Colloquium, May 13, 1991, as cited in Dolores Hayden, *The Power of Place: Urban Landscapes as Public History* (Cambridge: MIT Press, 1995), 43.

3 A sampling of such criticism includes Fredric Jameson, *Postmodernism, or, the Cultural Logic of Late Capitalism* (Durham: Duke University Press, 1991); David Harvey, *The Condition of Postmodernity* (Cambridge, Mass.: Blackwell, 1990); Margaret Morse, "The Ontology of Everyday Distraction: The Freeway, the Mall, and Television," in Patricia Mellencamp, ed., *Logics of Television: Essays in Cultural Criticism* (Bloomington: Indiana University Press, 1990), 193–221; Michael Sorkin, ed., *Variations on a Theme Park: The New American City and the End of Public Space* (New York: Noonday Press, 1992); Edward Soja, *Postmodern Geographies: The Reassertion of Space in Critical Theory* (London: Verso Books, 1989); and M. Christine Boyer, *The City of Collective Memory: Its Historical Imagery and Architectural Entertainments* (Cambridge: MIT Press, 1994).

For a feminist critique of some of these urban spatial theories, see the two essays by Rosalyn Deutsche, "Men in Space" and "Boys Town," in her *Evictions: Art and Spatial Politics* (Cambridge: MIT Press, 1996), 195–202, 203–244. For a specific critique of Michael Sorkin's position, see my "Imagining an Impossible World Picture," in Stan Allen and Kyong Park, eds., *Sites and Stations: Provisional Utopias* (New York: Lusitania Press, 1995), 77–88.

4 Henri Lefebvre, *The Production of Space*, trans. Donald Nicholson-Smith (Oxford: Blackwell, 1991), 52.

5 Lucy Lippard, *The Lure of the Local: Senses of Place in a Multicultural Society* (New York: New

Press, 1997), 7. Much of Lippard's thinking is informed by the work of cultural geographer and landscape historian John Brinckerhoff Jackson. See his *Landscapes* (Amherst: University of Massachusetts Press, 1970); *The Necessity for Ruins* (Amherst: University of Massachusetts Press, 1980); *Discovering the Vernacular Landscape* (New Haven: Yale University Press, 1984); and *A Sense of Place, a Sense of Time* (New Haven: Yale University Press, 1994).

6 For instance, see Martin Heidegger, "Building Dwelling Thinking," in *Poetry, Language, Thought*, trans. Albert Hofstadter (New York: Harper & Row, 1971), 143–162.

7 Lippard, *The Lure of the Local*, 7.

8 Yi-Tu Fuan, *Space and Place: The Perspective of Experience* (Minneapolis: University of Minnesota Press, 1977).

9 Christian Norberg-Schulz, *Genius Loci: Towards a Phenomenology of Architecture* (London: Academy Editions, 1980), and *The Concept of Dwelling: On the Way to Figurative Architecture* (New York: Rizzoli, 1984).

10 For instance, Marc Augé, *Non-places: Introduction to an Anthropology of Supermodernity*, trans. John Howe (London: Verso Books, 1995).

11 This kind of thinking is consistent with the ideas behind "new urbanism," an approach to architecture and urban planning that opposes the density and scale of centralized cities and, its counterpart, suburban sprawl. New urbanists advocate the development of architecturally and socially controlled small towns in which one can ideally walk between work, school, and home. On new urbanism, see Peter Katz and Vincent Scully, Jr., *New Urbanism: Toward an Architecture of Community* (New York: McGraw-Hill, 1993); Kenneth B. Hall and Gerald A. Porterfield, *Community by Design: New Urbanism for Suburbs and Small Communities* (New York: McGraw-Hill, 2001); and Peter Calthorpe, *The Next American Metropolis: Ecology, Community, and the American Dream* (Princeton: Princeton Architectural Press, 1993). The planned community design of Andrés Duany and Elizabeth Plater-Zyberk, especially Seaside in Florida, is an important, though controversial, test project.

12 James Meyer, "The Functional Site," *Documents* 7 (Fall 1996): 20–29, and "Nomads," *Parkett* 35 (May 1997): 205–214. See also the discussion in chapter 1.

13 On related points, see David Deitcher, "Eviction Notice," *Documents* 11 (Winter 1998): 46–54.

14 Don DeLillo, *Valparaiso* (New York: Scribner, 1999).

15 Here is a sample of such "communication" in which Majeski is being interviewed by telephone:

> Yes. This is Michael Majeski. Hello, ABC Australia. Yes. I understand we are speaking live. What time is it there? No. What time is it there? Yes. I'm learning Spanish on tape. Yes. Some stranger had crept inside, like surreptitiously, to eat my airline food. No. The moment does not whisper the usual things. No. She brushes her teeth with baking soda. Yes. When I saw the towering mountains capped with snow. That's when I realized. Yes. That's when I realized. No. It was hugely and vastly comic. He had an unnamed rare disease. Pick up the white courtesy phone, please. Yes. But first I'm at the breakfast table staring at my eggs. No. What day is it there? No. What day is it there? Yes. When I saw the towering mountains capped with snow. That's when I realized there was something terribly, terribly, wrong. No. She jerked me off in a taxi once. Yes. I was treated wonderfully, wonderfully well. They called me Miguel. (DeLillo, *Valparaiso,* 34)

16 See Jameson, *Postmodernism, or, the Cultural Logic of Late Capitalism,* 26–27.

17 Copy from the dust jacket of *Valparaiso.*

18 DeLillo, *Valparaiso,* 32.

19 Ibid., 86–87.

20 Ibid., 88.

21 Gilles Deleuze and Félix Guattari, *A Thousand Plateaus,* trans. Brian Massumi (Minneapolis: University of Minnesota Press, 1987).

22 Frampton, "Towards a Critical Regionalism," 21.

23 Homi K. Bhabha, "Double Visions," *Artforum* (January 1992): 88.

INDEX

Page numbers in italics indicate illustrations.